AMISH
Reflections

Heart-warming Glimpses of the Simple Life

JOYANNE TOTH HAM

For additional copies visit your local bookstore or contact:

    Clay & Joyanne Ham

    768 Ragersville Road

    Sugarcreek, Ohio 44681

    joyanneham@tusco.net

Pictured on the cover:

Emma Lou and Melissa Beachy

Design by: Rosetta Mullet

Carlisle Printing

OF WALNUT CREEK LTD

800.927.4196 · carlisleprinting.com

Sugarcreek, Ohio 44681

Dedication

This book is dedicated to the "Miller Sisters," who welcomed me into their family, and despite my faults they loved me, accepted me, forgave me, and showed me I Corinthians 13 love. I hope I can live up to the example you have each set before me. Though I have used an author's discretion and changed some of your names to protect your privacy, **you know who you are!**

To *Mommie* and *Daudi* who did such a
Godly job of raising those sisters.

Also to Serena Miller, without whose encouragement
and help this book would never have been written.

And to my Logophile, Bibliophile, Punctuation
Wizard daughter, Anessa,
Thank you.

But mostly, to my husband, Clay.

Amish Reflections

Introduction

I don't pretend to be an expert on the Amish. I especially don't pretend to know all the facts or their history. When my husband Clay and I moved to Amish Country from Texas in 2000, we did not know we would be opening a Bed & Breakfast in Sugarcreek. We also did not know how close to the Amish we would become. We did know that we were endeavoring to follow what we believed was a leading from God. I now know that by becoming closely acquainted with an Amish family they have changed my life forever, simply by being Amish.

If someone asked me to describe Amish people I would say: They are honest, hardworking, thrifty, friendly, God-fearing people who are quick to laugh and just as quick to forgive. They are equally as slow to gossip about, slander, or judge others, whether the others are Amish or *Englich*. At least that is true of the Amish I have been blessed to know.

Amish love God, life, children, hard work, ice cream, going barefoot, noodles, cleanliness, pretzels, horses, applesauce, laughing, cinnamon rolls, and gardening. Not necessarily in that order.

I admire their dedication to God. I do not believe that they have all the answers, but their methods certainly rate our attention and possibly imitating. To dedicate their whole lifestyle to God seems so unique, yet isn't that what any Christian is supposed to do?

I love being around them. Watching how they treat each other. Watching how they play with their children, touching and teaching, showing and sharing, making every child know he is loved and important. Watching how the women respect their husbands. Watching the reverence shown to the elderly. Watching the sibling love instead of sibling rivalry. Watching the young people planning a life together with divorce not being an option.

They have taught me how to be more patient with others, how to get up and get going when the job needs doing, how to give and receive help, and best of all, how to laugh at myself and allow others to laugh at me. Like their children, through their total acceptance of me, I am beginning to feel loved and worthy.

This book is my tribute to the love and acceptance I have been given. In it I hope to show you my *Amish Reflections*; my thoughts, my laughter, my awe at their everyday way of life.

Contents

Things that make me smile

Shiny black buggies, pulled by black horses with heads held proudly, high-stepping out of the past and into my present.

Hauling Amish

Shortly after moving to Ohio, when Clay was still working at a local cheese house, one of his Amish coworkers asked him, "You don't like working here, do you?"

"No."

"Then why don't you haul Amish?"

"Haul Amish?" Being a Texas boy, the first thing that flashed through his Texas brain was a picture of a semi truck, with its trailer loaded down with cows, *Hauling Cattle* down the highway.

After deciding that this picture couldn't be correct, he asked, "What do you mean, *Haul Amish?*"

"You get a 15-passenger van, get your name out, and start a taxi service for Amish people."

How could we ever have imagined the world this would open up for us?

Because Amish have chosen to use horses and buggies instead of automobiles, there are times when they need to go farther than a horse and buggy can go, or times when they need to get there sooner than using a horse and buggy could achieve. At these times they hire a driver who charges them by the mile to drive them wherever they need to go.

Amish Joke: *(Told to me by an Amish man.)*

Question: If half of the world were Amish, what would the other half be?

Answer: Drivers for the Amish!

Like many of us, most Amish are frugal with their money, thus the 15-passenger van is necessary. They arrange a Hauling. They plan a Hauling. If they can get others to go with them, sharing the trip, then they will also share the cost. If they cannot get enough people to go with them, they will simply cancel the trip. So they ask neighbors if they would like to go along. They ask their relatives who they haven't seen in a while, giving them a chance to also visit. After several stops, the van is full, and we are on our way.

Another Amish Joke: *(Also told to me by an Amish man.)*

Question: How many Amish can you fit into a 15-passenger van?

Answer: One more!

Since they are paying to go all the way to Dover, Wooster, Canton, or wherever a doctor or dentist appointment might be, they might as well do some shopping and get their money's worth.

No matter how many stores or shops they go to, almost always Wal-Mart is on the list. Now that our fleet of vans has grown to two vans, and we can drive in separate directions, driving separate groups of people, it is not unusual for Clay and me to find ourselves both waiting on the Wal-Mart parking lot at the same time.

"How long have you been here?" Clay may ask me.

"Oh, only about 15 minutes."

"Then we've got time. Let's go have lunch together," he'll invite.

How many hours have we spent sitting on a Wal-Mart parking lot waiting for Amish to shop? I am of the opinion that no Amish lady can come out of a Wal-Mart in less than two hours. There's a whole world of interesting items in a Wal-Mart that are not a part of her everyday life in the Amish community. Looking at all of these takes time. She can't decide by watching TV which brand is best, so she must read and study containers. They might run into someone they know, and will take this opportunity to visit, as spending time in Wal-Mart is easier than hitching up the horse and buggy and traveling to visit someone. If there is a place to eat in the store, why not visit over a sandwich or a cup of coffee? Then, as they may only get to go to Wal-Mart about once a month, there will be a large amount of groceries to buy.

I use this time to balance my checkbook, work on crafts, or write *reflections* about the Amish. Once Clay has finished any shopping I might have asked him to do, he usually catches up on his much-needed beauty rest.

When they come out of Wal-Mart, with their carts loaded, another fun time begins. Remember, the van is full of people to save on the cost of the trip. Where are we going to put all these groceries? Some plan ahead by inviting less people to go along, and request that we remove a bench/seat. (If we only had $1.00 for every time that seat has been pulled out and put back…) This leaves a big space to fill with groceries. If not, groceries are put under seats, beside seats, on laps, and anywhere they will fit. Spaces are quickly filled and the last persons to finish shopping may have to hold many bags on their laps, and put groceries between their feet on the floor.

Wal-Mart is almost always the last place they want to go, as they can usually finish up shopping there for whatever they could not find elsewhere. One time when Clay was finishing up a Hauling and heading toward Wal-Mart, the lady he was driving interrupted him by saying, "I don't need to go to Wal-Mart!"

"You don't need to go to Wal-Mart? Are you sure you're Amish?" he asked in surprise.

She laughed!

Picking up passengers for the trip is frequently a challenge. "It's the third farm on the left," they tell you over the phone.

They may not have a phone in their home, but nearly all Amish have phones at the end of their property, in little shanties that resemble outhouses. Phones can be used for business, emergencies, or to make appointments. Spending time just chatting on the phone is discouraged. Of course weather conditions help with the discouragement. Who wants to sit and chat in an unheated, unair-conditioned booth that you had to walk through snow or rain to get to? Many times a phone booth will be shared with one, two, or more neighbors.

"The third farm on the left? Do you know the house number?"

"No, it's the one with the big white barn."

Great! That eliminates half of the farms in Holmes County. The ones with *red* barns!

One, two, I count as I drive down the road. Is that a farm? Could it be just a house?

I can always stop and ask, as Amish communities are close enough that everyone knows their neighbor.

"I'm looking for the Yoder house."

"Well, there's Eli Yoder, and Mose Yoder, and Samuel Yoder…"

Did I forget to mention that about one third of the Amish in Holmes County are "Yoders"?

Third Amish Joke:

Question: What do you call a van that drives Amish?

Answer: A Yoder Toter!

Once I have found Eli Yoder's house it will be easier from there on. Eli can direct me to the next place, the next place, and so on. We'll pick up some here, drop off children there to be baby-sat, pick up another couple elsewhere, until I am totally confused and lost.

Amish Arithmethic Problem:

1st stop: 5 people get on—2 adults and 3 children.

2nd stop: 3 children and 1 adult get off; 1 adult gets back on.

3rd stop: 2 adults and 4 children get on.

4th stop: 2 adults get on.

5th stop: 2 adults and 5 children get on.

6th stop: 4 adults and 9 children get off.

7th stop: 3 adults get on; we return to stop #6 and 4 adults get on.

How many people are on the van?

If you answered 11, you are wrong! You forgot the driver!

One of the first things they often do after getting on the van is ask about the weather.

"Is it going to rain?"

"How cold is it going to get tonight?"

They know that we have radios, TVs, and the Weather Channel, and we are therefore likely to have a more accurate forecast than their newspaper or Farmer's Almanac. As many of them are farmers, the weather is an important topic of conversation.

We are also often the carriers of news. Frequently I know before they do when their aunt is in the hospital, or their cousin has had her baby, or that little Caleb has broken his arm, as I was the one who drove them to the hospital. I have even been the one to tell them that they are related to someone.

"He told me he was your father's cousin."

"I didn't know that."

Most Amish are related one to another; so close-knit is their community. I know four couples that are married to brothers and sisters. Let me explain: Example 1: Her brother is married to his sister. Example 2: Her sister is married to his brother. Now I get confused here! Does that make the children's parents also their aunt and uncle? Are their siblings also their cousins? Is it possible that they are their own cousin? Every time I try to figure this out, I just get more confused and a little dizzy. Once when Sarah and I were counting her cousins she confessed, "I don't know if I count Paul's children once or twice." *(See example 1 above.)* At last count, Sarah has 73 cousins just on her mother's side.

We have been driving Amish for so long now that I have had the pleasure of watching their children grow up before my eyes. Our children grow up with automobiles as a daily way of life. Amish children may go weeks without riding in an automobile, much less a large van that holds 15 people. The younger ones, who have not gone to school yet and learned English, cannot understand me or talk to me, so they are shy and keep their distance.

Laura, who had just learned to walk, repeatedly took one look at me, then toddled to the back of the van as fast as her little unsteady legs would carry her. "You can't get me from here," her face seemed to say. She would only come forward to sit with her Mom after much persuasion.

Her cousin Josiah was always the opposite. He would be the first child out of the house, toddling toward the van as fast as he could, then climbing up steps that were much too large for his tiny body, but he saw no obstacle in those steps. He was going for a ride in the big van no matter what it took. There was adventure ahead and Josiah was going to be a part of it.

Arlin hesitated and stood a few feet back from the van door each time. He was intrigued. The boy in him was interested in the machine, but the fears of a two-year-old were just a little stronger. He enjoyed riding in the van until the day he became car-sick. For a long time after that he looked at me as if *I* had caused his sickness.

Many of these children climb on board carrying their own empty plastic butter tub or a Cool Whip bowl with a lid, which they can use if the car-sickness becomes too bad. If they are small, Mom carries a bowl for them. I carry spare containers and paper towels, just in case.

Most Amish children love to go in the big van, but don't get to go every time. Large families make children take turns, leaving room for cost-saving co-riders and groceries. Like our children, they remember whose turn it is, but all disappointment seems to have disappeared by the time we return home, as they run out to greet the van, diving into each bag, seeking what new treasures might have been bought. It still surprises me how easily they are pleased with the seemingly smallest gifts.

I've watched teenage girls, in the back of the van, checking out boys along the road as we go along, pointing and giggling like all girls their age. It hasn't occurred to them that I can watch them in my rearview mirror. I've heard them talk about their hair, how it won't stay straight, or is too curly, or even how they are having a "bad hair day." (How can you tell under the *Kapp*?) I've even heard them discuss which *Kapp* is the prettiest.

With "Hauling Amish," as with any other occupation, there are good days and there are bad days. I remember one morning that I thought I could make an early morning drop-off, then get back to serve breakfast to my Bed & Breakfast guests. To start off with, I couldn't find the first house. "Second house on the left…"

"Yeah! Could that possibly be the house…way up over that hill?"

Okay! Now we are off to the next stop. No? We have to go to the bank? Naturally, the bank is in the opposite direction of where we need to be!

The second stop is no problem. Whew! Maybe I *can* get back in time to get that Breakfast Casserole out of the oven before it becomes a large brick.

The third stop? No one told me there would be a third stop. I was told two stops. That's why I thought I could do this before breakfast. Oh, the third stop is on the way, and just down the road…at the end of that *long* drive which is presently blocked by a truck with a trailer. There is no option but to pull into the parking lot of the small engine shop across the road and wait, *patiently*, until the owner of the truck with trailer finishes his business.

Ahh, the truck is beginning to leave. I start my engine, begin to pull out of the parking lot, then see the horse and buggy which has begun its slow process *down* the long, narrow drive which I need to drive *up*. This seems like one of those unique times just made for "counting our blessings."

The happy ending to this story is that Clay arrived home from his hauling before me, removed the Breakfast Casserole right on time, and was serving and entertaining our guests as if he didn't even need me.

It's hard to forget the night Katie left Jason on the van. Clay laughs about it now, but at the time he was not happy. He was on his way home, late at night, thinking about his bed and sleep when, "Ring! Ring!" his cell phone rang.

"Hello!"

"Clay, this is Katie. We think we left Jason on the van."

"You're kidding!"

"No! He's not here! We can't find him!"

"I can't see anyone on the van."

"He was sleeping on the backseat. Can you go back and look for him?"

"Okay. Hold on while I pull over…and walk to the back… There he is! Sound asleep. Do you want him?"

Katie laughs.

Okay, so Hauling Amish isn't always an ideal occupation, like the time I drove all the way home from Akron, late at night, in the pouring rain, with a baby screaming right behind me, but it has given me a thousand "I'll never forget" memories, such as:

1. We were driving along when suddenly from the back of the van came music. One of our passengers began playing a harmonica. He entertained us for quite some time. Another time a little girl asked me to, "Turn on the music machine." *(The stereo.)*

2. I laugh every time I recall overhearing about the "discussion" the Amish man had with the Jehovah's Witness over whose religion was "correct." I would have liked to have been a fly on the wall to hear that discussion.

3. Taking a family to a wedding, I asked, "Is it an *Englich* wedding?"

   The lady sitting up front with me answered, "No, Mennonite."

   "Aren't Mennonites *Englich*?"

   After thinking for a second or two, she replied, "They're halfway in between."

4. Every time 3-year-old Leeann saw a "Hauling van" pass her house she would call out, "There's our van." If her parents asked her, "Who's our driver?" she would reply, "Clay Ham."

5. When people ask us to haul on Sunday, we reply, "We don't usually drive on Sunday, except for emergencies." The Amish man on the other end of the line paused for a moment, then asked, "My wife is in labor. Is that considered an emergency?" It was!

6. "See that goat staked on the side of the road? Do you know what that is?" I fell for it and asked, "What?"

   "That's an Amish Weed Eater." Fanny replied with a big grin.

7. An elderly Amish gentleman, when asked a question, answered, "All I know is what I read in the *Budget*." (Wasn't that the *Times?*)

8. An Amish person who has left the Church, or chosen not to join the Church, is said to have "jumped the fence." Driving past a field one time, we noticed a cow that was outside the fence, beside the road. Thinking we might need to try and find the owner so that the cow could be put back to safety, I asked, "I wonder who owns that cow?"

   "Well, it can't be an Amish cow," my rider said.

   "How do you know that?"

   "Because she's 'jumped the fence.'"

It's easy to smile when I remember these conversations and look forward to tomorrow's Hauling. Where will I go? Who will I Haul? I may not know the answers to those questions, but I do know that with each Hauling I become more and more intrigued with "their world" and less and less comfortable with the *Englich* world."

And be not conformed to this world: but be ye transformed by the renewing of your mind, that ye may prove what is that good, and acceptable, and perfect, will of God.

Romans 12:2

Things that make me smile

Waiting in the van as mothers strap their infants into car seats, movement in my side view mirror catches my attention. Like a small television screen, a whole landscape, painted in vibrant autumn colors, is perfectly framed for my enjoyment. The movement that caught my attention, a horse and buggy, trots elegantly from one side of the mirror to the other. When it's over, I want to push rewind.

January

Most of the shops and restaurants were closed, but the post office and the banks were open. All of the small country schools were closed, but the bigger schools in the towns and villages were holding classes as usual. There seemed to be extra buggies and extra 15-passenger vans on the roads, but not any extra regular traffic.

Was it a holiday? Only to the Amish. It was Old Christmas. On the 6th of January, the Amish celebrate another Christmas, which they call Old Christmas.

To me it seemed like just another opportunity for Amish families to gather together, visit, and eat, which they love to do anyway. As I drove them on that frosty morning, I began asking questions so that I might learn if there wasn't something else to this tradition of Old Christmas.

"It is a day to keep holy," my passenger answered me. "A day to consider the true meaning of Christmas. A day spent differently than the other Christmas. There are no gifts. We only do necessary chores and we fast until the noon meal is prepared."

No gifts? Fasting? A Christmas of giving and no receiving? What an interesting concept.

The grass sticks through the snow. There has been very little snow so far this year, yet nearly every Amish child I see walking to school this morning pulls a sled behind him. Lunch pails and whatever else they might need for that day are piled on the sled. There is fun ahead, come recess.

No school bus for these Amish children. Mom will not drive them in a heated car. They will walk to the local, one-room schoolhouse, the way children have walked to school for hundreds of years.

One group of children is different. Every child is dressed in the traditional dark clothes, including black bonnets for girls and black hats for boys, but unexpectedly, in this one group I see an array of colors. Scarves of purple, pink, baby blue, white, mint green, and rose are carefully wrapped around each child's neck. Were they Christmas gifts, lovingly made by Mom? In the middle of what is often a dull world, these beautiful, bold colors of children's scarves against their dark and black clothing are making an Amish quilt.

I crest the next hill on my way to pick up Rachel, and the slumber of winter lies before me. In every direction I look, the fields, the trees, the barns and houses, and even the fences seem to be asleep. How do I know? Every fence post is wearing a nightcap of white. Peace stretches before me; mile upon mile of white, quiet, undisturbed, still peace.

I feel sorry for the tourists who come during the rush and bustle of summer and autumn and miss this tranquility. Pulling off to the side of the road, I sit for a moment or two and just relax and enjoy. It was very early in my Amish Hauling career that I learned that no amount of money could buy these moments. When everything in my world is moving too quickly, when problems seem overwhelming, I can simply pull over, sit, breathe, look, enjoy, and whisper, "Thank You, Father." You have to whisper. You don't want to wake up the fence posts.

Later that evening, when I am bringing the ladies home, we notice one lone boy making his way home. His face is rosy with the cold, but he wears a smile. The ladies listen while I tell them how the boy reminds me of coming home as a child, and opening the door to warmth and good cooking smells and safety and love. Is there any feeling better than that, when you are a child? How I envied that boy, for now as the wife and mother I am the one who makes it warm and good smelling.

From the back of the van, Rachel's great-aunt says, "I remember us kids, walking home from school. When we rounded that last curve in the road, we could smell it. I can still smell it. Mom would be singing. Mom was always singing and cooking. She would take sweet potatoes, 'slice them thick,' and fry them in butter. Then she would put them in a roasting pan, sprinkle them with a little brown sugar, and put them in the oven. That was what we smelled as we came around the curve; sweet potatoes baking in her old wood-burning cookstove. The sweet potatoes would bake in the oven until we got the milking done. Then we could eat them. Oh, they were so good."

Morning Coffee

"What do Amish ladies do in the winter, when you have no garden to tend, no fruit or vegetables to put up, and no lawns and flower beds to take care of?" I asked the Amish lady I was driving.

After a moment's thought, she answered, "We do a lot of sewing. It's also a good time for quilting. Some might want to do some cleaning that there just isn't time for at other times of the year."

Quilting, special cleaning, and even sewing are an opportunity for a get-together. An Amish barn raising is not the only time Amish get together to work and help each other and just have fun. The Amish family I know will use any excuse to gather together, eat, visit, and do whatever work needs doing. They call it a *frolic*.

When women get together for a quilting, sewing, or cleaning, they will start early in the morning. They want to finish in time to be home for older children returning from school, and in time to prepare dinner for their husbands. Many times they will get up early enough to do laundry and bake something to take with them, for before the work begins, they will have a "Morning Coffee."

My first pickup is Rachel. Rachel is small, with dark hair and glasses, but those glasses can't hide the eagerness and excitement, with just a touch of mischief that seems to always shine from her eyes. Rachel has a "Peter Pan" aura. She is light and sprightly, with a "never-grow-up" attitude. Being in her presence is nearly always fun. Yet when I grieved the loss of my Dad, her presence and her mint tea helped heal my heart. She is carrying a bowl I recognize from other Morning Coffees. It will be full of fresh fruit: grapes, bananas, pineapple, and whatever else is available this time of year. Very little, if any dressing, is used, just healthy, delicious fruit.

We drive through Farmerstown to pick up our next passenger. Because it is Tuesday, and Farmerstown is hosting its weekly "Trade Days," we must wait behind a line of buggies which are turning into the auction. The back of the buggy just ahead of us is piled high with cages. Each cage contains a rabbit. To our left are two boys in a small open buggy. They seem hardly older than ten or eleven. There are two pet carriers stacked between them and a third carrier rests on one boy's lap. The carriers contain puppies, to be auctioned off. The boys seem too young to already be entrepreneurs, but Amish children, though sheltered in some ways, are taught responsibility at a young age. Raising rabbits, puppies, chickens, or even goats is a good way for a young Amish boy to make some extra money. How I would like to see how much they get for their puppies, but once the traffic clears, we must continue on.

Deborah gets on next. Deborah is one of Rachel's older sisters. She has lighter colored hair that, much to her dismay, tries to frizz when the weather is *dreab*. (*Dreab* is an "Amish" word that Deborah has tried, in vain, to define for me, many times. She says it is not cloudy, or dreary, or misty, but *dreab*. As when it is just about to rain. Instead of saying four words, you can say *dreab*. But she claims that still does not quite describe *dreab*. Maybe you had to grow up Amish to understand all that.) Deborah loves life as much as Rachel but has a more serious, questioning attitude about her. She is inquisitive, always ready to ask and go and do. Her love of family is as strong as her love of life, and though she is always ready to go, she is often the first one to suggest we start home. Her suggestion is always met with much teasing and name-calling. She is carrying something that starts my stomach rumbling—her sausage gravy.

At Deborah's stop, we also pick up *Mommie* (the "Amish" word for grandmother), as *Mommie* lives in Deborah's *Daudi house*. (*Daudi* is the "Amish" word for grandfather. A *Daudi house* is a smaller house, usually next to the main house, where grandparents live after all of their children are grown.) How does one describe *Mommie*? She is little, without an ounce of spare flesh, nimble, and active, always doing something, especially for someone else, and always has a sweet word for me. Do I smell banana bread? Nearly everything *Mommie* bakes has bananas in it.

Ruth is picked up after that. Ruth is the oldest of the sisters. She never bosses us, as most older sisters would. We think of her as the quiet, peaceful, patient sister. We also think this group needs a quiet, peaceful, patient sister. After my Dad passed away, it was also beside Ruth, on her porch, that I sat for tranquil spells, drawing from her peaceful nature. Ruth brings with her the unmistakable scent of her cinnamon rolls. Boy, am I glad I am always asked if I want to join their "Coffee."

As each sister is picked up, the chatter grows louder, the laughter is more frequent, and the aroma of fresh-baked goods is almost more than this driver can endure. They talk among themselves, sometimes in English and sometimes in their mother tongue. Most call it Dutch. It is not Dutch; it is a form of German (*Deutsch*). I call it "Amish."

Americanized over hundreds of years, many American words are used such as "Bacon Cheeseburger" and many German words that are pronounced differently than they would be in Germany.

These ladies want to be polite and include me in the conversation by speaking English, but get excited, or need to think about something, or just forget and slip back to their own language. Each time they realize they are excluding me from the conversation, they apologize and return to English for a while. I tell them each time that it does not bother me; I understand it is hard for them to talk English all the time, and not all the people I drive are as considerate as these ladies.

One time, while not in the van, I was sitting behind Deborah, so she didn't realize I was there. In "Amish" she said, "We don't have to talk English. There is no one *Englich* here."

The others pointed to me, for her to see, and told me what she had said. They speak English so well that it always surprises me that it is difficult for them.

They talk about the things women have talked about for hundreds of years: children, family, household chores, gardens, canning, and laundry.

"Look, Abby has her laundry out!"

"I got mine out!"

"Oh, I didn't have time! Mine will have to wait until tomorrow."

I'm sitting there quietly thanking God for my automatic washer and dryer, especially the dryer on a cold day like this. I can't imagine hanging out clothes in the snow!

No "liberated" woman has convinced these ladies that they are not fulfilled in their simple lives. To me they seem far more contented than the *Englich* women I know. (To the Amish, anyone who is not Amish is *Englich*.) The simplest things please and excite them. The hardest work doesn't seem to bother them. But then, any time there is a big job to do, sisters, cousins, aunts, or neighbors will work with them until the job is done, knowing when they need help, these same people will be there for them. To the Amish, family and community are extremely important.

Just down the road, and over the next hill, we come to a quick stop. The road is full of cows. A farmer and his daughter are moving their cows from one field to another. I turn off the van engine. We are going to be here a while. The lead cow takes one look at this big white van in the road, moves to her right, and keeps going, seemingly undisturbed. Other cows don't handle it quite so well. They look worried and try to turn around to avoid this big white object, which was not there only a minute ago. With some persuasion from the farmer and his daughter, the cows are made to continue in the proper direction. We wave to the farmer and his daughter as they and the last cow pass by and we are on our way again.

A little farther down the road our obstacles are human. Buggies are parked all along the side of the road. Amish in Sunday clothes of black and white, carrying "potluck" dishes, walk along the road.

"Church on Tuesday?" I ask.

"They are ordaining a new minister. It will be an all-day service."

Why will it be an all-day service? As well as ordaining a new minister, they will have communion.

Prior to this day of communion, they will have a preparatory church service known as council meeting, in accordance with their interpretation of I Corinthians 11:26-34. Each individual must confess to being in agreement with the standards of the church and profess a desire to partake of communion. This is usually done on a one-on-one basis with one of the ministers.

If someone is guilty of a serious sin of offense, the person must ask forgiveness of the church as a whole. When forgiveness is asked, it is almost always given. "Then he shall be forgiven and it shall be talked about no more."

The Amish lady who was explaining the above quotation to me said it in a singsong fashion, indicating how many times she had heard it. To me its beauty was unforgettable, and I thought worthy of more awe than her tone denoted. What a truly beautiful attitude to have. *"Then he shall be forgiven and it shall be talked about no more."*

If a member has a grievance with his neighbor—say his neighbor's cow keeps getting out and trampling his garden—then this grievance must be resolved. Some grievances might take some discussion or suggestions before a solution can be reached. If everyone is not in agreement, this could take a while. Communion will not be taken until all grievances are settled, and everyone is considered "worthy" to partake of the communion according to the Scriptures listed previously.

Finally we reach our destination, Katie's house, and all pile out of the van. If you looked up "laughter" in the dictionary, you would see a picture of Katie. Katie laughs almost continuously, and at almost anything. Her face glows with her contentment. How could anyone be unhappy around her?

The last two sisters are already there. Lydia has come by buggy, as she lives only a short distance from Katie. Anna has hired another driver.

Lydia is the third sister, small in stature, like *Mommie,* but taller than Rachel. She always makes a point to greet me, was the first sister to ever hug me (an outward display of affection not often seen among Amish), and was the sister who taught me that it was safe to laugh at myself and be laughed at by those who truly love you. Lydia is the mother of Jordan, whose story you will read later on in this book. I believe it describes the heart of Lydia better than I can do here in a few words.

The baby sister, Anna, works hard to not be thought of as the baby. Though I've never heard her use the word *dreab*, she has hair like Deborah's, and I've heard stories of how angry it made her as a child. She seems to have outgrown her anger, or perhaps she has replaced it with fierce determination. Does that come from survival, being the youngest of 12 children? Her determination is positive, however—always channeled toward making something better. Anna is aggressive, starts something, and often gets the others to follow her lead. A fanatic about healthy food, she is the gardener in our group and would rather be outside digging in the dirt than anyplace else. Fortunately we often benefit from her gardening endeavors, whenever something produces in great abundance.

The house is warm and inviting, and smells of yet more great dishes which Katie, Lydia and Anna have prepared. There is talk of cleaning, for after we have Coffee we are going to clean. Looking around the house, I try to see what we will clean. It all looks clean. Before the day is over I will learn that there are things and places to clean that I didn't even know could or should be cleaned. But first we will have Coffee.

Now, "Coffee" is not just something to drink. This Coffee will be all the enticing foods I have been smelling for about an hour—fruit, juice, coffee, and about two hours of talk. Yes, we will work, and we will eat, and eat, and eat some more, but the best part of a Coffee or a *Frolic* is the opportunity to visit. Without phones or cars, these occasions are fun fellowship times. They never seem to tire of each other's company. The love, though very rarely spoken of, is tremendously obvious in their actions.

While the children run and play, and have to be convinced to stop playing long enough to eat, the women just enjoy, or is that love, each other. I, the only *Englich* person in the group, am truly blessed to be included.

Therefore all things whatsoever ye would that men should do to you, do ye even so to them.

Matthew 7:12

Ruth's Easy Cinnamon Rolls

2 cups very warm water
⅔ cup vegetable oil
½ tsp. salt
5 Tbsp. instant potato flakes
6-7 cups bread flour
2 Tbsp. yeast
⅔ cup sugar

2 eggs (beaten)
1 Tbsp. vanilla
1 Tbsp. cinnamon
¾ cup brown sugar
butter
icing (to taste)

Mix all together, except cinnamon, brown sugar, butter, and icing. Let it rise until double. Mix together cinnamon and brown sugar. Roll dough out and spread with melted butter and cinnamon-brown sugar mixture. Roll up. Cut ½" thick. Bake at 350° until lightly brown. May be iced when they have cooled.

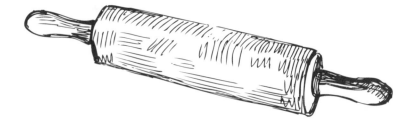

Things that make me smile

Quiet misty mornings, when the mist clings to the low places in the fields. Trees seem to be floating. Cows seem to be standing in a cloud. Everything seems somehow to be at peace.

February

Was I really complaining just last month that there hadn't been much snow? What was I thinking?

Two weeks ago the first of three snowstorms blew in. Snowflakes at least an inch in diameter crowded the sky. Blowing from the east, I wondered if this was what the old-timers called a Nor'easter. Having never watched such a storm before, I sat down at the window and enjoyed the performance.

After a couple of hours, of more huge snowflakes blowing than even God could count, my enthusiasm began to turn to worry. Clay had a Hauling later that night. He couldn't possibly go out driving in this, but he couldn't call them to cancel, as they didn't have a phone in their home. Just as we decided that worrying was not a good option, our Hauling for that night called us. They had been watching the snow also, wondering if Clay would come or if they even wanted to go out in such a storm. By mutual agreement, it was decided that the Hauling for the night should be canceled.

Now there was nothing left to do but build up the fire, make some hot chocolate, and enjoy a cozy evening together, watching the snow fall.

The next morning we awoke to an enchanting world of white. Snow has such a democratic way of making everything, whether clean or dirty, pretty or ugly, rich or poor, all pure white and equal.

As soon as the roads were plowed, we were off again, trying to Haul Amish. Now the problems will be snow-covered lanes or driveways and snow piled in farmyards. Turning around a 15-passenger van in these tight spaces is difficult in the best of weather, but in winter it can become impossible.

If the ice and snow are too bad, the Amish will readily volunteer to walk out to the main road. One time Rachel left a sled at the end of her lane. Knowing her own shopping habits, she planned ahead. When I dropped her off, she piled all of her purchases onto the sled and pulled it home, instead of carrying it all the way up her long lane.

The weatherman has predicted that a warming spell is coming, so Amish children are ice-skating before the ice melts.

"You better skate tonight," I overheard one mother tell her children. "Tomorrow is supposed to be warmer."

Remembering the night we took a van load of young people to ice-skate is one of those memories you want to store somewhere, so you can pull it out when things don't look too good and you need something pleasant to think about.

It was already dark by the time we had finished picking up everyone and arrived at the destination. I will never forget the sight that met my eyes as we came around a corner in the road. Like a scene from an old black-and-white movie, we were transported back in time. There before my eyes was spread the snow-covered valley. Nestled at the bottom was the pond, frozen and surrounded by snow-covered trees, looking as if they belonged on a Christmas card.

On the pond were dozens of skaters. Two lights, run by generators, lit the pond. There was even a barrel with a fire burning in it for kids to warm themselves when they were not skating. Very few kids stood near the fire, in spite of the temperature being only about 20 degrees; in fact, many of the boys were skating without their coats on.

I got out of the van so I could walk over to stand and watch for a while. I thought that I could stand and watch this enchanting scene forever. The sight of the skaters going round and round in clothes reminiscent of costumes of more romantic times long past was better than any TV program, far more beautiful, and ten times more peaceful. There was no music blaring, as there would be in any of our skating rinks; just nature and the sounds of the skaters. No matter how much I longed to stand and breathe in this atmosphere, I quickly became so cold that I had to go back to the van and turn up the heater.

My chickens are so funny. They will hardly come out of the barn because of the snow. They step into it, pick up their feet, and hold them in midair, looking at them, not knowing what to do next. I miss them running up to the patio, searching for table scraps. Is there anything more funny than a chicken running?

The Benefit Auction

What is the name of the man for which the Benefit Auction is being held? I don't know. He is Amish. He has cancer. He needs the help of his people, and when one of their own needs help, Amish will pull together and do whatever is necessary. I have seen this done time and time again, but never on such a large scale as this night.

Earlier in the evening, my husband, Clay, left to take a van load of Amish to the benefit. We had planned that he would drop them off, then wait for them. I had another load of people to take to a different destination. After I dropped off my people, I would pick them up later in the evening, which gave us a few hours in between to meet at the benefit, eat dinner, donate to a worthy cause, and just enjoy the event.

At least two or three miles from where the benefit is to be held, the traffic increases. Buggies travel on the shoulder of the road, not just one every now and then, but one after another after another. Dozens of other families walk together, holding the hands of younger children and carrying babies. Some ride bicycles, others drive small carts or pony traps, and still others have hired vans to take them.

"Tonight a benefit is being held at Keim Lumber in Charm, Ohio, to help one of their own, and they come from all directions to help, to give, and to enjoy." A scene from the movie *King of Kings* flashed through my mind. I see the multitudes coming from all directions to hear the Sermon on the Mount. As they came then, they come tonight.

I am almost immediately amazed at the organization. We've all heard of, and many of us have seen films and pictures of an Amish barn raising, but what about an Amish Benefit Auction?

Even before I reach the parking lot, I am directed by one of many teenage boys as to where I should park. Then signs lead us, pointing the way. Who made all these signs? Who placed all of them in the appropriate places? Who organized the boys as to how to park cars, telling them where to stand and where to have us park?

Inside the building thousands of people are already working, eating, walking around, visiting, and just enjoying themselves. Ten rows of folding tables, spanning at least 40 yards, are filled with people eating barbecued chicken, potato salad, Amish noodles, applesauce, and pie. Additional tables have been set up in a different direction for food service.

Who decided who would cook what? How many women did it take to cook all this food? With the exception of the chicken, the food would all be donated, cooked in private homes, then brought to the benefit. The chicken would be barbecued by men. How was it all transported here? Who set up all of these tables?

Church wagons line one wall, giving evidence as to where all the benches came from, but who set them all out? Who would put them all back in the church wagons when the benefit was over and transport them back to where they would be needed on Sunday for church?

Hundreds more benches and chairs are set up on the other side of the building for the auction that is already taking place, and still people are standing because there are not enough places to sit.

We walk through one of six food lines, where one person hands us a tray, one puts a plate on the tray, one gives us plastic silverware wrapped in a napkin, the next person gives us half of a barbecued chicken, and so on down the line until our trays are completed. Everyone has a job, and no matter how small it may seem, no one is made to feel inferior, put out, or unappreciated. They each do their job and we pass through the line quickly.

At the end of each table is a large white box marked "DONATIONS." All of the food lines are staffed by women. The donation boxes are watched by men. They were older men who perhaps would have trouble with harder physical work, but their dignity has been preserved with this important position.

At once a man appeared at our side, "You can sit over there, row three, room for two." Another job has been done promptly and efficiently.

The chicken is good, the potato salad is excellent, the noodles are truly Amish, and the pie is definitely homemade. We eat our fill and move over to the auction area.

All the merchandise to be auctioned off is displayed in an area to the left of the auctioneer. There are tables, chairs, and a hutch; all fine furniture made of hardwood. A ladder, jars of salve, boxes of eggs, pillows, pictures, fishing rods, and items too many to list await their turn on the auctioneer's block. It is obvious that everyone has given their best, be it a bentwood rocker or two dozen cookies wrapped in a pretty box. I am reminded of the Widow's Mite.

How did all these donations get here? How did people know that they needed to donate? Who displayed them all so nicely?

We find seats and join in the auction. A quilt goes for a surprisingly low $300.00. A box of cookies gets a delightful $35.00. The auctioneer was going when we came in at 6:00 p.m. He was still going strong at 7:45 p.m. when I had to leave, and the merchandise on display seemed hardly touched. He was selling fast, about an item every 45 seconds. They ranged from ten dollars to hundreds of dollars. How much money can that be? Would it be enough? I didn't know.

I say something to the Amish gentleman seated next to me about how much money is being made. His reply is, "He needs it!" We strike up a conversation and before it is over he has one of our Amish Hauling business cards and wants to know if we could take him to a doctor's appointment on Monday.

The auction goes on. People are still eating, though many have switched to bowls of homemade ice cream, being offered at yet another table with its own donation box. You can add your own chocolate syrup or eat it plain. I enjoy mine plain so that I can taste every bit of the homemade flavor.

There is a constant murmur of conversation in the air. As Amish don't have as many opportunities to get out and visit as we *Englich* do, they are talking and visiting more than they are buying. It seems as if everyone knows everyone else. An auction to them is obviously more entertainment than business.

Adults sit for hours in the same place, watching, listening, talking, and laughing. Children, well behaved as usual, sit beside them. A little girl, two rows up from us, quietly eats her ice cream while looking around at all the activity. When she is done, she scrapes and scrapes the bowl with her spoon. Is she truly still hungry, or has it become a toy to entertain her? Her little brother became restless and Dad takes his turn at holding him for a while. I marvel again at how well behaved Amish children are. We have been there over an hour, and those two children, and many others, have been there as long or longer, yet they sit quietly amusing themselves.

All too soon, the time comes when I must reluctantly leave to pick up my Amish passengers and return them to their home. I leave feeling a little better than when I came, hoping others feel the same way. We gave and we received. We ate an excellent meal, we enjoyed ourselves, and hopefully one of our own had his medical bills paid, was healed, and returned to the people who love him.

Give, and it shall be given unto you;
good measure, pressed down, and shaken
together, and running over.

Luke 6:38

Benefit Potato Salad

3 cups cooked & shredded potatoes
3 hard-boiled eggs (shredded)

½ cup celery
onion to taste

Dressing:
¾ cup salad dressing (Miracle Whip)
1 Tbsp. vinegar
½ cup sugar

1 Tbsp. mustard
1 tsp. salt

    Shred or chop and mix together potatoes, celery, eggs, and onions. Mix dressing ingredients and stir into potato mix. Let set for a couple of hours before serving to enhance flavor.

    (This recipe has been cut down to family size. Much larger proportions would be needed to take to a benefit, frolic, or family gathering.)

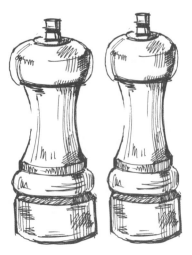

Things that make me smile

He is pure white. He is big. He has a bright red comb and wattle. He doesn't walk; he struts. What is this rooster saying? "Who do you think owns this barnyard?"

March

I saw ground today for the first time in weeks. Snow has covered it for so long that I had almost forgotten what ground looked like. The snow that we so longed for only weeks ago has become tiresome. No longer pristine and white, everywhere it looks dusty gray and there are so many muddy brown piles.

It melts sooner where our footprints and the animals' footprints are, giving evidence to wherever we have been walking all these weeks. I wonder how long it will take for all this piled-up snow to melt.

The chickens flap from one bare spot to another, still not wanting to step in snow if they don't have to. They search diligently at each bare spot, hoping to find something to peck at. The expression "Slim Pickin's" takes on a new meaning to me.

Driving along, I pass fields that still look like miles of pure white, untouched, sparkling snow. On my left I see footsteps that cross a huge field, then climb up a hill and disappear from my sight. I wonder where they were going, walking such a distance in what has to be knee-deep snow. Was it an adventure, a quest some child took on, or had Mom sent him on an errand to the next farm?

The crocus have appeared, as if by magic, overnight. Lavender, white, and yellow, with their spiky, dark green leaves against the snow, they seem to be announcing, "Spring is coming! Don't give up! Spring is coming! We bring the promise of all the colors to come."

March winds turn the old windmills, making them creak and groan. March winds fan out the hair on the horses' tails and manes, making them look as if a blow-dryer has been used. And March winds bring to my nose the scent of freshly plowed earth as farmers who plow with horses instead of tractors begin to turn over the earth, preparing it for the next crop.

There is life in every field. Calves, colts, kids, and lambs are testing out their new, wobbly legs and wondering about their new world, but always remaining safely close to Mom.

On my way to pick up Mary one morning I happened to catch the cutest sight. In one field, with his nose right up against the fence, was a calf that can only be a day or two old. In the adjacent field, with her nose up against the same fence, is a lamb of about the same age. With the fence between them they can only sniff and look, but the look on their faces is identical and priceless.

"What are you?" one seems to be asking.

"What are *you*?" the other seems to reply.

There is another field that brings to mind a memory each time I pass by. Four cows and three calves were in this field. It looked as if I was driving past just as the three calves were awakening from a morning nap. While the calves slept, their Moms had wandered as they grazed, leaving the calves sleeping some distance away from them.

Now the calves found themselves sleepily looking around for lunch. All three calves walked toward the brown-and-white cow, as she was standing closest to them. The cream-colored calf recognized his mother and began his lunch. The remaining two calves, a roan-colored one and a tiny black one, looked around in confusion. They both took off together at a trot for the next closest cow, a brown one. The little black calf was at most only a few days old, still somewhat unsteady on his legs, and arrived at the brown cow in time to see Roan also begin to enjoy his lunch. Discouragement and confusion were clearly written on Little Black's face.

I watched him look to his far right to the one black cow that was way out in the field. Then he looked straight ahead about thirty yards to the second black cow. With all the practice of his few days of running, he took off toward the cow in front of him. No awards for gracefulness would have been awarded to him. His knobby little legs seemed to go in every direction. When he got to within ten feet of her, she looked up from her grazing but made no signal that I could interpret, to indicate that she was the object of his search. He continued walking; they touched noses, as if to say, "Hello." Little Black dove for his lunch, and Mom went back to hers. I sat and marveled at life, motherhood, and the God who made them all.

Some Amish ladies are already talking about planting their vegetable gardens.

"Can you plant this early?" I ask.

"Oh, yes! You can plant lettuce and cabbage," one answers.

"I've already got my peas and radishes in," another says.

Yesterday the water on my favorite pond was aquamarine blue and smooth as glass. Before the day was over, we on the van had to shed our heavy jackets, as the temperature climbed to 52 degrees. With the sun shining brightly through the winter air, it became pleasantly warm inside the van.

This morning as I pass the same pond, the water is murky gray and choppy enough to have its own little waves. It is 15 degrees. I doubt we will be shedding our jackets today.

Coming down the road toward me is a horse and buggy with a horse that has "frost whiskers." The warm air from his nose comes out in billowing puffs, like smoke from a boiler, hits the frigid air, and freezes on his face and ears. The longer he goes, the longer his frost whiskers grow around his mouth and also coming out of his ears. They are sparkling white like the flocking on a Christmas tree. Aren't they cold?

It is so cold that my Amish ladies come out wearing black head scarves over their head coverings. That is to say, the mothers are wearing black scarves. The younger girls, the daughters, must find the head scarves too old fashioned for their taste, for they are wearing only their white head coverings. Teenagers are teenagers. Looks are far more important than whether or not one is cold. *Mommie* is wearing the traditional heavy black Amish *bonnet* over her head covering as Amish have done for hundreds of years. Every culture seems to lose a little something with each generation, while the oldest generation tries gallantly to hold on to what they think is important.

They're plowing! Isn't it too wet to plow? Only the Amish are plowing, as it is too wet for tractors to get into the fields. But with horses, they can get an early start on the *Englich.*

As we drive along with my passengers, we see farmer after farmer plowing. This one has three horses; that one has four.

Amish are partial to Belgians, the breed of horse most popular in this area. They pull the plows through fields of stubble, left over from last year's corn crop. Heads down, shoulders bobbing, strong muscles taut, these massive, golden-colored beasts work in almost perfect unison. Ugly fields of stubble become precise lines of plowed earth, the color of chocolate. It always reminds me of when you take a vegetable peeler to a block of chocolate to make curls for decorating a cake. The farmers are making row after row of chocolate curls.

Yesterday I saw six big strong Belgians hooked to one plow. As I drove by, they waited patiently as their owner, on his knees in the dirt, made some adjustment or repair to the plow. I wondered at his fearless attitude. If those six horses jerked forward, he could be seriously injured by the plow, but they stood obediently, waiting, resting.

After picking up my passengers, we returned back along the same road and I saw that the farmer had finished his repair and was again plowing; horses straining as they have done for hundreds of years to ready the earth for yet another crop.

Bird-Watching

It's 5:30 on a cold morning in March. It's 28 degrees and it seems to take forever for the van to warm up. How cold can a steering wheel feel, even with gloves on? We are going Bird-Watching. I consider asking my passengers, "Are you sure that the birds are awake?" I envision birds, cozy and warm in their little nests, perhaps even with a tiny quilt on top of them. After all, isn't this Amish Country? Instead I keep my sleepy, wildly imaginative comments to myself.

We drive through the darkness for what seems like hours. Could it only seem that way because I'm still half asleep? Have I ever told you that I am not a morning person?

Finally we come to our first stop. It is a lake near Perrysville. Wow! Was I wrong! The sun has managed to climb out of his bed, tossing aside *his* quilt, and is casting a weak, somewhat sleepy light across the lake. The lake is covered with all kinds of waterfowl. They are not only awake, but are loud, and happy to be alive.

My Bird-Watchers, two men, one girl, and nine boys in sizes from about seven years old to boys in their teens, pile out of the van and head for the lake, enthusiastically carrying equipment used to make the watching more enjoyable. They seem unaware that it may be light, but it is still *cold*!

I am left to sit in a van which quickly begins to lose the heat I so eagerly enjoyed just a short while ago. As I sit, my fingers growing colder, I gaze at the wonder of a sunrise on a lake. Dark silhouettes of trees and bushes turn from black to brown and green. Clouds of pink and orange and yellow gradually turn white, on a pale blue winter sky. The dark mass of water, the lake, turns from phantom black to winter gray. A fluttering in a nearby tree catches my attention.

Wow, again! There in the tree right next to my van is a pileated woodpecker! (I had to look that up later, in my field guide, to know what his name was. Did you think I came up with *that* name off the top of my head?) I have never seen one of them before. (Understandably, the field guide lists them as "uncommon.") He looks like Woody Woodpecker. The pileated only stays for a minute, then he is gone, leaving me with the thought, "Huh, maybe Bird-Watching could be fun, but couldn't we do it a little later in the day and when it is a little warmer?"

The Bird-Watchers climb back into the van, putting back all that heavy equipment, and give me directions to the next stop.

Different bird names are called out as we drive along. I figure out what is happening. As someone sights a bird, they call out its name and everyone looks expectantly in the proper direction. None of the names they call out sound even vaguely familiar to me, and I have not sighted one of these unusual-sounding birds, even though I try to look expectantly in the proper direction. My sighting is hampered somewhat by having to drive, but I do see some birds and consider calling out, "Sparrow!" "Cardinal!" "Robin!"

One of the younger boys has a device which plays birdcalls. As we drive along, we are periodically entertained with unusual birdcalls coming from the back of the van. Not once do I hear a sparrow, a cardinal, or even a robin.

We continue moving from one place to another, dragging out all of the equipment at each place, setting it up, watching birds for a period of time, then packing up all of the equipment, returning it to the van, and continuing on to another place. I have no idea how they know where to go, or how they know where the birds will be. I just drive as I am directed.

By about the third stop, our four youngest boys seem to have had enough Bird-Watching for one day. They find an interesting bridge at one stop, and a bubbling creek at the next stop. With just running and exploring in little-boy fashion, they have contentedly replaced Bird-Watching. There are no cries of "I'm bored!" which we have grown accustomed to with our children. In Amish-children fashion, they are completely self-amused.

A few stops later I am in for a pleasant surprise. As I pull up to park, I recognize that van! Clay is parked here! He too is driving bird-watchers. We have an enjoyable little visit while bird-watching goes on. Eating our packed lunches together makes it seem like a winter picnic.

I'm not sure how my Bird-Watchers handled the situation, but at one point I had to drive off, find a gas station, and use the public restroom. Oh, the fun of driving Amish!

Just as I thought the day must be over, and surely we would be going home soon, someone, in another group of Bird-Watchers, told someone in my group, that they had sighted a white-winged scoter. Oh, joy! Such rapture! Over a bird? Off we go, returning to a place where we had stopped earlier in the day, to see the white-winged scoter!

Finally, we are indeed headed home. My picnic lunch is but a fond memory, so I begin thinking about what I can prepare for dinner. One of the smaller boys says, "Mom said she would make Chicken

Noodle Soup for supper." He goes on to sing his Mom's praises, describing how good her soup is, and in the process making us all extremely hungry. When he is dropped off at his house it is all I can do to not go inside with him, sit down at the table, and look hungry and pitiful until I get my bowl of sympathy soup.

I arrive home to a cold, empty house. (Clay is not home yet.) There is no Chicken Noodle Soup bubbling on my stove. Opening a can just doesn't seem quite adequate.

Clay arrives home, asking, "Did you see the eagles?"

"No! Did you see eagles?"

"Yes! They asked me if I wanted to look through their telescope at some bald eagles. There were two of them sitting right beside their nest."

"Well, we sighted a white-winged scoter!"

"A what?"

"Never mind. How about if we go out to eat at Beachy's Restaurant for dinner?"

I happen to know that Beachy's makes a great Chicken Noodle Soup.

Bless the Lord, O my soul, and forget not all his benefits...
Who satisfieth thy mouth with good things; so that thy
youth is renewed like the eagle's.

Psalm 103:2 & 5

Mom's Chicken Noodle Soup

3 cups diced & cooked chicken
1 cup diced & cooked carrots
1 cup diced celery
2 quarts chicken broth
1 can cream of chicken soup
 (That doesn't sound very Amish!)

1 tsp. parsley
1 tsp. chicken flavoring (can be found in bulk food stores)
1 tsp. salt
4 cups cooked noodles

Mix all ingredients. Bring to boil. Serve with fresh-baked bread.

Things that make me smile

Young colts running for the sheer joy of running, slowing down and pausing only when they must turn at the fence, then running again, kicking out their back feet, or raising up their front feet, with their tails and manes flowing out behind them, proclaiming to the world, "I'm alive, I'm free, and I'm lovin' it!"

April

It must be spring. Everywhere I look the world is waking up. First it was a haze, or a mist that seemed to surround every treetop; just a hint of color of what is to come. Red, yellow, orange, lime green, and even chartreuse hovers like clouds around each tree. Then all at once it seems with only one warm day, blossoms burst forth, covering trees. It looks as if popcorn has popped on every branch and twig, white and fluffy and breathtaking.

Then it happened again. Every year it happens to me. Everywhere I look, suddenly it is green. Every year I watch, trying to outfox spring. Surely this year I will catch the point in time when it all turns green, and again every year I am caught off guard, and suddenly everything is green. When did it happen? How did I miss it? Again?

Driving on this spring morning, I see daffodils—hundreds of them in a patch of woods behind a house, and another patch of them—on a bank, growing wild beside the road. Who planted them there? Was there once a house there, years ago, where some woman lovingly planted bulbs and excitedly waited for them to shoot up then bloom in the spring?

Wasn't it in April that the tornado went through? Some said it was not a tornado, just high winds. I lived in what is called "Tornado Alley" from 1962 until 2000. I know what tornado damage looks like. When only one tree in a row of trees is plucked up, that's a tornado. When metal is twisted, not just blown over, that's a tornado. When one house loses it roof, and the one right next to it is almost untouched, that's a tornado.

It went through on a Thursday, but I didn't see the results until Saturday, when I was asked to drive some of our neighbors to Mt. Hope. They were going to help their family whose roof had been damaged in the tornado. When I went back that evening to pick them up, they asked if we could drive through the path that the tornado had taken.

There, before our eyes, dozens of trees that had been plucked up were already cut into firewood-sized logs and neatly stacked alongside the road. Small branches had been hauled off to burnpiles. Destruction had been sorted into neat piles; twisted metal here, usable wood there, burnable wood over there.

Tents were set up, with women serving food and drink to the volunteer workers. A bulldozer was preparing the land where a barn had once stood, and soon a new one would stand. Temporary repairs and patches were already done. There was a house that had its siding replaced, and there was another whose roof had been replaced.

On and on it went, repair after repair. Nowhere did I see any one sitting beside the road complaining about the government, saying, "When are they going to do something for us?" Everywhere I saw people happily working, helping each other, doing whatever they could to make the situation better. Amish don't rely on the government. They rely on each other. I often wonder if the rest of the world held this attitude, how much more effective and complete would our lives be?

Everyone's rhubarb is taller than mine. They are all pulling rhubarb and making pies, custard, cobbler, and ice cream topping, while I am still wondering why I did not get some horse manure from one of my Amish families and put it on my rhubarb plants last autumn. I have still not pulled any!

Mommie had pity on me and gave me a bag of rhubarb, all cleaned and cut up. She must wonder why I can't grow my own. Perhaps I could if I had a horse on hand that produced nice fertilizer and I didn't have to transport horse manure in a closed van. (If you do that, be sure to use a container with a lid. Phew!) Oh well, maybe next autumn I'll get it done.

Now they are plowing in earnest. Not just an occasional, eager farmer, but in nearly every field we pass, they are plowing. There are three horses, there are four, and over there in that distant field are five horses, all with heads bobbing up and down in their own private rhythm.

I remember the morning we dropped off Rachel's youngest girl at *Mommie's*, and passed the field where six Percheron horses were plowing. It was early morning and they were fresh, rested, and eager to work. They stepped lightly, with heads held high, proclaiming the dignity of their breed.

As chance would have it, we returned that afternoon just as those same six horses were returning to the barn after a day of plowing. Those same proud horses now plodded along with heads hung low. Every step they took with those huge feet was slow, full of effort, and all signs of dignity were lost to fatigue. When they reached the barn they stood patiently waiting for their harnesses and bridles to be removed. The second the bridles were removed they darted for the water trough, thrust their noses deep into the water, and drank thirstily.

Before anyone could stop him, two-year-old Josiah jumped off the van and ran over to stand and watch the horses being unhitched. No one but me seemed concerned over this tiny child standing so close to these giant horses. In Amish thinking, it was simply natural for this little boy to be getting accustomed to horses in his life.

What I didn't know was how gentle these giant horses can be. I watched in horror, another time, as a team was led from a barn, where in the doorway sat three tiny kittens. My horror turned to amazement as I watched the horse that was next to the kittens gently put his feet down, missing all three kittens.

Calves, colts, lambs, and kids that stayed close to Mom only days ago are now jumping, running, prancing, and gamboling a little farther away from Mom each day. If I pull off to the side of the road to enjoy their antics, as soon as they spot me they dash for Mom, then peek out from behind her, with that same question on their faces, "What are you?"

The Amish man I drive the next day has a comment for nearly every farmer that he sees plowing. "Oh, he's got five horses."

"He's only got three."

"He's got two plow blades, but he's only using one. Huh?"

I think the four acres and house my passenger is presently living on is not enough for him. Like most Amish men, he wants to own a farm.

Then he says something that catches my attention. Something about "resting at the end of the row."

"What does that mean?" I ask.

He explains that the farmer lets the horses rest a short while at the end of each row before beginning on the next row. This allows him to plow much longer without the horses getting too tired.

"Resting at the end of the row," I think.

We could all use a little more "resting at the end of the row." In our busy non-Amish world, how often do we take a minute or two to "rest at the end of the row"? Didn't God rest at the end of the week? I wonder, could we go longer, not tire out so easily, and perhaps be a little more patient with those we love, if we could "rest at the end of the row"? And perhaps while we are resting, we could take a minute to enjoy the new green leaves, the popcorn blossoms, and the daffodils.

Mommie's Rhubarb Dessert

Crust:
1 cup flour   ½ cup butter
2 Tbsp. sugar

Filling:
5 cups rhubarb   7 Tbsp. flour
3 egg yolks   ½ tsp. salt
1½ cups sugar   ½ cup cream

Meringue:
3 egg whites   ½ tsp. salt
½ cup sugar   ½ tsp. cream of tartar

    Mix together crust ingredients and press into baking dish. Bake at 350° for 10 minutes. Mix together filling ingredients, pour over baked crust, and bake for 45 minutes. Whip egg whites with salt and cream of tartar until stiff. Add sugar. Put on top of filling and bake an additional 10 minutes. (This recipe was given to me with very little instructions. I have added what I thought was necessary for a successful dessert.)

Funerals

We buried my Daddy on a cold April day. I hadn't called him Daddy in years, yet suddenly I could call him nothing else.

The night before, it rained all night. I awoke several times, envisioning all of us standing in the freezing rain beside his grave. Praying, I asked God to stop the rain, at least for the length of the graveside service.

By morning the rain had stopped, but the sky was heavily overcast, drizzly, and it was so cold. Hurrying out the door at the last moment, I almost didn't take a sweater or coat, not realizing how cold it was. How glad I was later that I had at least grabbed a sweater.

Since he had passed away in Texas, the funeral had been held there. There would only be a graveside service in Ohio, where he would be buried.

We pulled up to the graveside. On the left were American Legion men, older men, in uniform, standing with rifles at their sides. Their flags flapped briskly in the wind that blew harder on that hilltop cemetery than in the valley below. They waited patiently, willing to perform this service for a man they had never known.

My father was that kind of man. In a heartbeat he would have been one of them, standing in freezing drizzle, no matter the discomfort, ready to show honor and respect for one of his own.

In the center were the canopy, the chairs, and the flag-draped casket. There were clips on the flag to prevent it from flying off in the constant strong wind. Behind the row of chairs stood my Amish friend Mary, huddled within her coat against the bitter cold, which I knew bothered her so badly. She held a single red rose, and upon hugging me, she scolded me for not being dressed warmly enough, then handed me the rose.

Three American Legion men stood under the canopy with the priest. In the distance I noticed a man dressed in a dark tan overcoat. He seemed to be visiting another grave.

To the right was the sweetest sight I had seen since this entire nightmare began. In the confusion of grief, at first I didn't recognize them; a quiet group, all dressed in black, meekly standing in the drizzle, not under the canopy. The first one I recognized was Ruth. Then I realized who they were. My Amish friends, who had not known me for very long, had ventured into the unknown of an *Englich* funeral, to pay respects to a man they hardly knew. They had willingly joined our unfamiliar, worldly customs because of our friendship. Seeing them standing there brought on my first tears. There was *Mommie*, Ruth, Deborah and Henry, Reuben and Rachel, Regina and Carrie, and Paul. No other children, just the two girls I knew best.

The priest began the service after we were seated. The American Legion men read and were as much a part of the service as the priest. My eyes were constantly drawn to the seven men who stood quietly waiting in the freezing drizzle without the protection we had under the canopy. How old and frail they looked. Were they about my father's age of 82? I could not look to the right. Seeing my Amish friends would have made me cry again.

Prayers finished, they began to fold the flag. In the distance, the sound of bagpipes began to play, "Amazing Grace." The Captain of the American Legion handed my mother the flag, saying some quiet words to her that I could not hear. Mom, in her polite British manner, whispered, "Thank you."

By direction of the Captain, the guns were fired in their twenty-one-gun salute. The same salute as is given to any president was given to my father. My daughters, my mother, and I wept. A hand from behind patted me lovingly on my shoulder. It was Mary.

The gun salute completed, the sound of "taps" being played on a bugle came from the distance. I looked up, and slightly to my right, I saw the man in the dark tan overcoat that I had thought was visiting another grave. He stood at least a hundred yards off and it was he who played taps. Slowly, mournfully he played while I thought of all the times my military father had "gone to rest" to the sound of those notes. This would be the last time for him, but a first for me.

I was fifteen when they shot my then hero, President John F. Kennedy. Ever since that funeral, whenever I heard taps, I saw again Arlington cemetery, Jacqueline Kennedy's veiled face, and the eternal flame. Now, whenever I heard taps, my mind would be brought back to a cold, drizzly, windy hilltop cemetery in Ohio. I would forever see that lone man in the distance with the bugle to his mouth; those dedicated, loyal, older men standing with guns at their sides in the freezing drizzle; Mary with a single red rose waiting for me; and my Amish friends all dressed in traditional Amish funeral clothes, huddled quietly, reverently together, also in the freezing drizzle.

Four years later I attended my first Amish viewing. I no longer called them my friends. They were now my sisters. There was no official adoption, just an understanding of closeness that comes with time and caring. It is their brother's viewing that I must attend.

I felt awkward, out of place, and afraid I would do something wrong and make them wish I had stayed away. How could I stay away? I knew Jacob from all the family gatherings Clay and I had been blessed to attend.

To this day, when I hear the name Jacob I can see his face, round and full and smiling. Was he always smiling? And laughing? Jacob loved to kid and joke and laugh. The sisters are always telling stories of their childhood and how Jacob was always teasing them or pulling some prank.

How was it possible that all that joy had been snatched from our midst? What could this *Englich* sister have possibly contributed to the viewing? Across my mind flashed a memory.

"A lone man with a bugle to his mouth; loyal, older men standing with guns at their sides; Mary with a single red rose; and my Amish family all dressed in black, standing quietly in the freezing drizzle on a hilltop cemetery.

They braved the *Englich* world to attend their first *Englich* funeral for me. I would brave their world and attend my first Amish funeral for them. Isn't that what sisters do?

Everyone is dressed in black; black dresses with black aprons, black suits and coats, and black hats and bonnets. Some of the younger girls have not covered their head coverings with the traditional black church bonnet, so the pristine white was a welcome contrast in a sea of black.

It was June and warm enough that some children were barefooted. How cute; black dress, apron, head covering with church bonnet, and yet barefooted.

I have waited in the van at viewings while people stand in line for hours. It is a solemn event to witness the respect and reverence the Amish show every one of their own. It is also another masterpiece of organization.

At each funeral orange cones and signs announcing "FUNERAL" mark the road so people driving past know to be cautious. There will also be signs directing where buggies should park and signs directing where vans should park while we van drivers wait for our passengers to walk through and pay their respects.

Until Jacob's funeral I had always dropped off my passengers, stayed in the van, and waited. Now, I would *have* to go inside. I followed the person in front of me, through the basement door, hoping they knew what to do.

The basement had been all changed to rows of church benches, upon which sat Jacob's family. Familiar faces, yet grief had somehow made them unfamiliar and almost unrecognizable.

I passed through a seemingly endless line of people, shaking hands, because that is what the people in front of me did, until I was pulled down to sit between Deborah and Lydia. My relief at being pulled down was short lived as now in a sitting position, people who passed by assumed that I was a family member and every one of them shook my hand as they passed. Person after person shook my hand until it began to ache.

I checked the time by a clock on the wall, counted how many people passed within five minutes, then multiplied that number by how many hours the viewing would last. I was astonished to realize that thousands of people would pass by in the two days before the funeral.

When the funeral was all over, somehow I found myself sitting with *Mommie*, Jacob's mother, outside the basement door. We talked of things that are not uncomfortable. Things that people talk about every day, not on funeral days. I was so glad to see her looking better than she had the day before, and to see her moving about. *Mommie* is always moving, doing, helping, and never sitting still. I had never seen her as still as she sat yesterday. It frightened me!

Suddenly men from the neighborhood walked up and began moving benches toward the church wagons. As Amish do not have church buildings, they take turns hosting church in their homes, barns, and shops. Everything needed for church—benches, songbooks, and even dishes for the meal served after church—fits into a wagon which is moved by horse from house to house as it is needed. If more than one wagon of benches and supplies is needed, a neighboring church will loan its wagon.

The men worked for about an hour, restoring the lawn and the basement to its original state. They took down and folded the canopy under which visitors had eaten lunch. They put away any item that was out of place. Then they began folding benches and putting them in the wagon. Each bench has its own place and like a giant jigsaw puzzle, the wagon was filled with no gaps left over. When they began returning items to the basement I asked *Mommie* how they knew where those items went.

"They were the ones who took them out," she said, as if this was the way it should be.

Perhaps it is.

Then I realized that these men, unasked, had appeared the day before yesterday, just as they had appeared today, and began the task at hand, setting up for a funeral and putting it all back after the funeral. In typical Amish manner, family, neighbors, church members, and the community do whatever is necessary, without being asked, without complaint, without pay, and with a cheerful attitude.

While the men finished their work, the women were in the house working. Before they left, the house would be spotless.

Her family, her church, or the community will not stop helping at the end of the funeral. If Jacob's wife needs anything in the months and years to come, someone will take care of it. Someone else will do Jacob's chores until other arrangements are made. Clay tried to join in on a lawn-care frolic being held to mow, trim, weed, and clean up the yard. He came home, saying, "There were so many men over there that they could only give me little token jobs to do."

Uncles and grandfathers will see to it that her children will have male influence in their lives. A bank account will be opened in her name, and anonymous donations will be deposited for her and her children. While driving her, more than once other people have paid her bill and asked us to not say who paid it.

An Amish man once told me, "If anything ever happens to me, I know my family will be taken care of." Jacob's family will be taken care of.

Days pass and Denial has been pushed out of the way by the funeral. There is no denying what has happened. Before I have a chance to realize it, Doubt nudges up against my faith. I don't remember inviting Doubt in. I invited in Denial, because I wanted to deny what had happened, but I did not invite Doubt in. Did he just slip in quietly as if he was wearing soft house shoes? Doesn't it seem like Doubt should wear heavy boots and stomp in shouting accusations against God? Instead he whispers in my ear, "God didn't answer your prayers." I want to listen to him. Isn't it true? Did God answer our prayers? I can't listen to him! To listen to Doubt I would have to deny God's faithfulness.

Finally, Doubt in my head is no longer whispering. Not only is he now loud; he is also arrogant. How did this happen? How did Doubt grow from slipping in quietly to being loud and arrogant? What do I do with this Doubt?

I remember a Scripture where God asks Job, "Where were you when I laid the foundations of the earth…? Who determined the measures of the earth…? Who shut up the seas with doors…?"

And I think, "How poetic, Lord, but I still hear Doubt."

Then I remember God telling Jeremiah, "If you return (give up this mistaken tone of distrust and despair), then I will give you again a settled place of quiet and safety…" (Jeremiah 15:19, *Amplified*). Isn't that what I want? "A settled place of quiet and safety"? A place where it is easier to hear God than it is to hear Doubt? Yes!

So, the same way I let Doubt into my mind, I will let Faith in. One thought at a time. One situation at a time. One day at a time. I will refuse to entertain Doubt by thinking about Doubt! I will instead think Faith, Peace, and Joy! I will refuse to feed Doubt by thinking Doubt! Instead I will feed Love, Patience, and Temperance!

I also remember something Job said to God: "For the thing which I greatly feared is come upon me, and that which I was afraid of is come unto me" (Job 3:25).

Was Job saying *he* was responsible for what happened to him? Therefore am I responsible for what happens to me? "…give up this mistaken tone of distrust and despair…"

Tomorrow morning when the sun rises again over the field of corn beside my house, in stunning shades of pink, orange, gold, and red, knowing who created such an awesome display, I will remember what He told Job. I'll choose to trust God, and Doubt will not be quite so loud.

When millions of stars sparkle in the sky tonight perhaps their beauty will inspire me to trust in the God who flung them into their patterns, turn to His Word, feed my Faith, and therefore begin to starve out Doubt.

When geese fly over my house, honking as they pass by, knowing by some miraculous ability which way is north and which way is south, I will have to consider how much more intelligent than I is the God who made each one of those geese. So even though I don't yet understand totally why some prayers seem to get answered and some don't, I'll choose to "give up my mistaken tone of distrust," and with that, I'll push Doubt a little farther away from me.

When Jeffrey takes his first steps and his Uncle Jacob is not there to celebrate with us, I'll choose to praise God, and not think of Jacob as "lost," for he isn't lost! Praise God! Because of Jesus' sacrifice on the cross, I know exactly where he is! And as we wait to join him, I will endeavor to find that "…settled place of quiet and safety."

And seek not ye what ye shall eat, or what ye shall drink, neither be ye of a doubtful mind.

Luke 12:29

Things that make me smile

Horses that stand head to tail shooing flies for each other. Do they know or is it just coincidence? Standing head to tail, when they both swish their tails they are both shooing flies away from the other one's face. Is there a Christian lesson here?

May

May slipped in so quietly this year that I hardly noticed that April was gone. Perhaps it was because April had been so warm.

There are not nearly as many dandelions this year. I can remember other years when driving along, looking out at the fields, I saw only yellow. Yellow as far as the eye could see. How lovely! We passed an Amish family yesterday picking dandelion blossoms to sell to a local winery. How many dandelion blossoms do you need to make enough wine for a winery? I can't imagine, but the whole family, even small children, were picking.

One year I got it into my head to make dandelion jelly. Clay and I scoured our front lawn for blossoms, and then pulled the dusty yellow petals off the stems. I made a "tea" with the blossoms, just as the recipe instructed me, mixed in sugar and lemon juice, cooked it, then before I put it into jars, I tasted it. It tasted like grass! Is this what it is supposed to taste like? I jarred it, labeled it, and put it on the "jams for sale" shelf in the Bed & Breakfast. All twelve jars sold, but I haven't been able to bring myself to make any more.

Ruth and her family had a baby goat they named Dandy because he so loved to eat dandelions. When they found out the hard way that he also loved to eat strawberries, lettuce, cabbage, and most anything else in their garden, they sold him.

It's officially "Mowing Season." Most places only have four seasons, but I believe we have more than four and one of them is Mowing Season. Clay seems to spend most of his waking hours mowing, weed eating, and grass trimming. The only thing that grows faster than the grass is the dandelions. They don't bother me though, and I have trouble understanding why so many people hate them. I honestly think they are pretty. To me they look like a small chrysanthemum.

Dandelions are not the only flowers I see as I drive along. Whites, pinks, blues, lavenders, and yellows greet my eyes alongside the road. I should take the time to learn the names of all these beauties.

The foals are so much older now, and steady on their legs. How I love to watch them run. I sat watching one run back and forth across a large field one day, for what seemed like ten minutes. He only slowed down and turned as he approached the fence, then, head down, he took off again, as fast as he could. Never seeming to tire, he only stopped when he finally saw me, then once again repeated the pattern of "run to Mom." Skidding to a stop, his head popped out from behind her, and he looked me over with eyes that were beautiful, dark brown pools of curiosity with just a touch of fear.

By afternoon, all running will have ceased and foals can be seen sleeping in undignified piles of foal flesh, looking more dead than just resting from the morning runs.

Clay and I, as usual, are a little behind in our garden. We have planted cabbage, lettuce, broccoli, and Brussels sprouts. (We only plant Brussels sprouts for Mom, as neither Clay nor I will eat them.) Our new potatoes and peas are up, but as I drive past other gardens I see peas so much taller than ours, and some even have blossoms on them. The last time my Amish sisters and I got together, Rachel was passing out bags of leaf lettuce. I would have to use incredibly small bags to copy her.

Clay bought three new hens. They are black, so it is easy to tell them apart from our other golden chickens. He came in the other morning and announced that the new chickens must be Amish.

"Why? Because they are dressed in black?" I asked.

"No," he replied. "Because they get up and get to work earlier, like the Amish. Every morning when I go to the barn, they are up and have laid their eggs, while the other hens are sitting on the perch with a 'Do we have to get up?' look on their faces."

A few days later he asked me, "Since they are Amish chickens, would you make them some head coverings?"

I assumed he was joking, but I answered him saying, "If you can figure out how to tie them under their chins (Do chickens have chins?), I will make them head coverings."

Driving down the road, I notice the different activities in each field. In the first field I pass, the farmer is making hay. His horses pull a gas-powered baler, which spits out neat, tidy bales. In the next field, the farmer is planting field corn. With his horses he pulls a device which holds the seed in yellow plastic buckets. I wonder how it works as compared to the modern planters used by the *Englich*.

Field number three brings us to a farmer who is disking his field, and in the fourth field the farmer is doing "manure management."

Yesterday we looked out at the fields beside our Bed & Breakfast and saw field corn sprouting up, about two inches tall. "That wasn't there yesterday," my visiting daughter says. "I was looking that way yesterday morning, and that corn was *not* there!"

As it does every year, it suddenly appeared, zillions of sprouts where it seems only minutes ago there was nothing but blank field. If you catch the rows at a certain angle, it looks as if someone has taken a chartreuse highlighter and drawn hundreds of parallel lines on the field. What talent it must take to plow and plant in such even, perfect lines!

Within a week the image of highlighted lines will be gone, and instead the rows of corn will look like Grandma's embroidery stitches, slightly fuzzy, yet even, precise, green stitches on a brown quilt.

Wasn't it about this time of year when I was driving John, his wife Miriam, and their son Joseph? As we passed a farm on the right, we saw four Belgian horses and two foals in the yard, between the barn and the house. With no fence to stop them, it was only a matter of time before the horses would put themselves in danger by crossing the road. John said something in "Amish" to Miriam. I didn't understand him, but I understood the situation.

"Do you want me to go back?" I asked.

Everyone agreed that we should go back. We all got out of the van, wondering what each of us could do to help. There was no answer to our knock on the door at the house, so we assumed that no one was home.

John and Joseph started walking toward the large, nervous horses. When one came toward Joseph, two thousand pounds of fast-moving horseflesh, he merely held up his arms and stood his ground. The horse turned and ran in the direction that Joseph wanted him to. At that point I decided the best way I could help was to return to the van. If two thousand pounds of horseflesh came running toward me there would be no trouble deciding who was in charge…Not me!

They discovered an open barn door, assumed this was how the horses got out, closed that door, and began putting horses in stalls. When John came out of the barn he was complaining that he had stepped in horse sh__. (This was the first time I had heard an Amish man cuss.) He further stated that he had put one of the foals in with the wrong mare.

"How did you know it was the wrong mare?" I asked in all *Englich* innocence.

"I didn't," he snapped. "But she did!"

And wasn't it also this time of year when driving down the road, I noticed the four boys by the creek? It wasn't very warm, but they didn't seem to notice. Their pant legs were rolled up, their feet were bare, and their faces were lit with smiles. They didn't notice the cold. They were going to have fun.

Three of them were on the creek bank, about to enter the water, while the fourth was already in the water, with a stick in his hand. What was he seeing? I will never know what caused such joy, but they reminded me of another time, passing an Amish school, where again something in a creek had caught the attention of the children. Just as we passed this group of happy, smiling children, one boy came up from the creek, toward the road. I can clearly see his face to this day. It wasn't just his mouth that was smiling. His whole body smiled! I gasped at the sight of his pure delight. When had I last felt such happiness?

It is a question I have chosen to repeat many times since, for what is happiness? Some say, "Happiness is a warm puppy." I say, "Happiness is a choice," or better still, *our* choice. Paul said in Philippians 4:11 that he had learned to be content in whatsoever state he was in. Perhaps it comes from living among the Amish for so long, or perhaps it comes from having a preacher for a husband, but whatever the reason, I am endeavoring to remember that boy's smiling face, and choose to be happy, whatsoever state I am in.

Mommie's Dandelion Gravy

3 cups young dandelion greens

4 slices bacon

¼ cup sugar

½ tsp. salt

2 hard-boiled eggs (chopped, optional)

2 Tbsp. flour

1 egg (beaten)

¼ cup vinegar

1½ cups milk

Gather greens, wash, and pat dry with paper towel. Fry bacon, reserve grease, crumble bacon, and set aside. In a saucepan, mix sugar, salt, and flour together. Add vinegar and beaten egg. Add milk and reserved bacon grease. Cook over medium low heat until thickened, and then add greens all at once. Stir until all greens are wilted. Add bacon. (If using hard-boiled eggs, add now.) Pour over pan-fried potatoes and serve at once.

(An interesting note: *Mommie* gave me this recipe with very little directions, or even precise measurements. I'm sure she has made this dish so many times that she thinks anyone else would just know how to do it. I wanted so much to include this recipe, but not offend her by asking her for better directions. So what do we *Englich* do when we can't figure something out? We Google it! There it was! Almost the exact same recipe, only with clear-cut amounts and nice directions for us not so talented *Englich* cooks. I hope that when *Mommie* reads this, she will understand.)

Isaac

The rooster that was hatched from an artificial egg

Isaac's mother was a little black hen with a heart's desire to be a mother, and so she began to sit on eggs. Not just her own eggs, but also all the other hens' eggs. I gently informed this little black hen that we had no rooster, and without a rooster her eggs would not hatch. She chose to ignore me and continued to sit on the eggs.

When we collected the eggs every day, she sat on the next day's eggs. She became very possessive and protective at collection time, squawking, pecking, and did you know that chickens could growl? I began calling her Broody. Get it, brooding hen, Broody?

Egg collecting was no longer a pleasant chore. Something had to be done. Something had to change.

On my kitchen windowsill, two artificial resin eggs were sitting in two eggcups. They looked and felt like real eggs. I suggested to Clay, "Why don't we try putting these two artificial eggs in a nesting box so Broody can sit on them until she gets over this nesting thing? The other hens can lay their eggs in different nesting boxes and we won't have to fight her every morning."

Clay thought the idea was worth a try. Hoping she wouldn't notice the difference and refuse to sit on the resin eggs, we put them into a nice, clean nesting box, then moved Broody to that box. As expected, she squawked, and growled, and pecked, and otherwise protested, but nonetheless, settled down to hatch her two artificial eggs.

A couple of days later, I got an idea for a joke. I went to visit an Amish lady that Clay and I Haul who owns chickens *and* a rooster. Swearing her to secrecy, I explained what I intended to do, and asked her for two fertilized eggs. She laughed and fetched the two eggs for me. Upon arriving home, much to Broody's dismay, I removed the now much nurtured and protected artificial eggs and replaced them with the two fertilized ones.

But…**I didn't tell Clay!**

Days went by. Nearly every day Clay made some comment about "Poor Broody" such as, "I feel sorry for that poor chicken, Joyanne. She's still sitting on those artificial eggs. She thinks they're going to hatch and of course they're not."

"You don't know that!" I replied. "That little chicken has faith that she can be a mother. You claim to be a man of faith. Let's just watch and see what her faith can do."

All of you women reading this can just see the eye rolling and head shaking I received for that statement.

Day after day went by with Clay making daily comments about "Poor Broody." Daily I reminded him that, "All things are possible to him, or in this case, her, who believes."

One day he came in announcing, "I'm praying for that little chicken. She looks bad. She hardly gets off the nest to eat or drink."

"That's good, Clay. With your prayers and her faith, we'll just see what God can do."

There was no answer, only more head shaking and eye rolling.

Then came the morning when Clay came running up from the barn, with eyes as big as… oh, shall we say, eggs? He stammered out, all in one breath, all run together, "There's a baby chick in the barn, Joyanne— What'd you do?"

"What did I do? What do you mean, what did I do? And how can there be a baby chick in the barn?" Can you tell that I was not ready to confess?

We walked down to the barn together, with me enjoying the moment, asking questions such as, "Is there really a baby chick in the barn? Clay, are you pulling a joke on me?"

"NO! You're pulling a joke on me," he answered without much enjoyment in his voice.

Upon reaching the barn, we discovered, there was indeed, the cutest little yellow and black chick ever hatched.

In time I did confess to "hatching" this plot, at the same time reminding Clay of the joke he had once pulled on me and how I swore I would one day get even with him.

It wasn't until the next Sunday, as Clay was talking to his family by phone that I overheard the part of the story where Clay saw the hatchling for the first time. He never actually told this to me. I wonder if he would have, had I not overheard him.

He said, "I was in the chicken pen, feeding and watering the chickens, when I heard, 'Peep! Peep! Peep!' I turned toward the noise, and a baby chick POPPED its head out from under Broody! I thought I would faint! In rapid succession the following three thoughts went through my mind.

"Am I seeing things?

"Well, I did pray. Maybe God has done a miracle.

"Joyanne's done something!"

There is a moral to this story, in case you did not catch it: The moral is, **"Faith works!"**

Though she was only a chicken, her faith worked. The Bible doesn't say that you have to be someone or something special for faith to work. It just says, "Faith works." She had faith to be a mother, and there was never a better mother on this earth. All of her love and attention was centered on that one chick. (The other egg never hatched.)

We named the chick Isaac, hoping he would be a rooster. All of our Amish friends laughed and thought we were quite silly for naming a rooster. Thus the name Isaac.

When God told Sarah she would be a mother, she laughed. Isaac means "laughter," and years after Isaac was hatched from an artificial egg, we are still laughing.

Proudly, I told the "Isaac story" all over Amish Country, with every van load I carried. They loved it and laughed with each telling.

"Will you tell the rooster story?" Nettie asked. "Emma hasn't heard it." And they would all laugh again as if none of them had heard it before.

More than once, Clay would be driving along with a van full of Amish, when from somewhere in the back of the van a voice would call out, "Clay!"

"Yes."

"How's Isaac?" and the whole van load would once again burst into laughter.

I'm not sure any chick received as much attention as did this one. We went to the barn several times a day, just to look at him, pick him up, and stroke him. He became accustomed to the stroking, especially at night when we would secure the hens for the night. He and Broody were sleeping together in a nesting box, instead of on the perch with the other hens. If we did not stroke him "good night," he would stick his head out farther and farther until we did.

Naturally, the nesting box became more and more crowded each day as Isaac grew. One night when I went to close the hens up for the night, I noticed that Broody was not in the box with Isaac. Looking quickly to the perch, I counted hen heads and realized she was once again back with the other hens.

"I guess you're grown," I told Isaac.

Isaac did grow to be a fine, beautiful, pure black rooster, who was a total gentleman. When scraps were tossed out, he would "cluck" as his mother had done for him, saying, "Here's food! Here's food!" and would stand back and let them eat first, with only two exceptions. If strawberries or french fries were tossed into the chicken pen, he ate his full share.

One of our B & B guests, when told this, went to McDonald's and purchased french fries just for Isaac. When she decided that Isaac did not get enough because of the quick, greedy hens, she returned to McDonald's to purchase a larger order. Another time, return guests showed up to check in at the B & B with french fries in hand, ready to feed Isaac.

Because all of our B & B guests had heard the "Isaac story" from day one, they were always interested in how he was doing. He became a feature in our yearly newsletter, *Oak Haven B & B—The Inn Times,* with his own section entitled "Isaac Update."

He was almost grown, yet we had not heard him crow. That spring, my grandchildren, Sarah Grace and Benjamin, came to visit. Benjamin had somehow acquired a small stuffed rooster that would crow when squeezed. With all of his four years of wisdom, he decided that Isaac did not crow yet because he did not know what it sounded like, not having another rooster to copy. Benjamin stood for hours beside the fence to the chicken pen, squeezing the stuffed rooster again and again, making it crow.

Isaac did not crow while Benjamin stood there, but crowed for his first time two days after Benjamin went home. I wonder…

Isaac was not only a gentleman, but also gallant and brave. I remember the time a hawk appeared in the chicken pen. By the time I saw the hawk, Isaac had hustled all of the hens under a bush and was standing in front of the bush, ready to do battle with the hawk. We scared the hawk off, but for days afterwards, any time even a sparrow flew overhead, Isaac herded all of his girls into safety, back under the bushes.

There is a difference of opinion as to why one night we found Isaac hiding in a bush next to the garden shed. I said he was hiding in fear from the weasel we had not yet been able to catch. Clay insisted that Isaac was camouflaging himself in the bush, readying himself for the attack on the weasel. You decide.

We hoped that one of the hens would again sit on some eggs as Broody had done and give us some chicks. Isaac certainly did his part, but those uncooperative hens never again would hatch a son and heir for our special rooster.

Sadly, we come to the end of the "Isaac story." The day after we had a frolic to paint the barn, he began acting ill. The only thing we could figure out was that he didn't like the color *red* we had chosen for the barn. We contacted the vet. (How many people call a vet about a rooster?) We administered medicine that the vet gave us. (How many of you have ever put medicine in a rooster's mouth?) Within two weeks he died peacefully in his sleep at the ripe old age of five.

The hens, fickle creatures, didn't seem to miss him much, but I know some human tears were shed, when no one was looking, for everyone knows one shouldn't cry over a rooster. I will forever remember the excitement I felt the first time he crowed, the way he would stick his head out to be stroked, his love of McDonald's french fries, the way he protected and took care of his hens, and the way his black feathers turned sparkly green when the sun shone on them. Most people probably think there are no chickens in Heaven. I happen to believe there will be at least one fine black rooster named Isaac.

Now faith is the substance of things hoped for,
the evidence of things not seen.

Hebrews 11:1

Things that make me smile

New-cut hay, lying in neat rows, drying in the fields. Harvest! Proof of God's goodness.

June

Warm days and cool nights. Soon it will be hot days and not so cool nights, but for now the weather seems perfect. After such a snowy, cloudy, cold winter, everyone seems to be enjoying the clear blue skies.

The cornflowers crowd each other along the roadside, long and weedy, but their pretty blue blossoms seem to reflect the color of the sky above. Every time I see a patch of them I laugh. Clay and I have a private war going on concerning cornflowers. I believe I am winning the war, but I can't boast about my victory. Every time Clay mows or weed eats, he leaves the cornflowers, thinking they are pretty. I agree that the blossom is pretty, but I think the plant itself is too tall, scraggly, weedy, and ugly. So every time I find a cornflower plant that he has so purposely mowed or weeded around, I purposely pull it up and toss it on the compost pile. He never seems to notice that they aren't there anymore, looking so tall, scraggly, weedy, and ugly. You won't tell him what I'm doing, will you?

It seems as if in every direction I look, as I drive, they are making hay. Small square bales, larger square bales, and largest of all, round bales. Often these largest round bales are wrapped in white plastic, looking like giant marshmallows. A horse-drawn mower is being pulled in one field. In another field horses pull a tedder, which flips and turns the hay to help it dry. Over there, the horses pull a gas-run baler which spits out nice square bales. Later, the whole family will come to pick up the bales. Children of all sizes and even Mom help to get in the hay. Small children will lift bales that seem as large as they themselves are.

They lift them onto a flat-bed wagon, where an older brother or *Daed* (Dad) stacks the bales while the horses wait patiently for their job—pulling the hay-loaded wagon to the barn. If the family only has one wagon, all may take a break at this point, until the wagon gets back from the barn, and they begin to load hay bales again. However, often neighbor helps neighbor or family helps family to get the hay in. With help will often come a second wagon and team of horses, so that as one wagon is being unloaded at the barn, another is being loaded in the field.

In yet another field I see a boy who looks no older than twelve years old, professionally handling a team of horses, cutting hay. Each horse is twenty times the size of this boy, yet they placidly obey him. While he works a man's job, his younger siblings are riding a pony trap up and down the lane. The pony must be happy to be running in the warm sunshine, for both children are pulling hard on the reins, trying to no avail to slow down this energetic animal.

The largest, round bales, require a front-end loader to lift them and place them on a wagon, or take them to the barn one by one. I wonder why some Amish are allowed such equipment, while others are not. However they do it, the hay must be stored in anticipation of the winter. Deborah says she has not seen her husband for days, but she further says that this is normal for Hay Season.

The corn finally looks like corn. The highlighted lines on the field and Grandma's fluffy embroidery stitches are gone. Now, the easily recognizable corn is tall enough to wave in the breeze. The other day, just as I crested a hill and caught sight of a field of not quite as tall corn, at just the right angle, the term "corn rows" popped into my head. It looked just like someone's braided hair.

The apples on our trees are as big as large grapes, and the pears are as long as my thumb. The cherries have all been picked. Well, all that we could reach. We can never reach the ones at the very top of the tree and graciously leave those for the birds to eat.

One would think they would be appreciative of our offering. They are not! The Resident Robins sit in one of the apple trees and scold us the entire time that we are picking cherries as if that cherry tree is their personal property. Not bothered by their scolding, I pick cherries with visions of cherry pie, sour cherry jam, and cherry-almond muffins. The muffins are a favorite of many of our Bed & Breakfast guests.

Deborah may think it is Hay Season, but I think it is Strawberry Season. So many signs on the side of the road boast, **"Strawberries—pick your own."** Amish children sit at makeshift stands selling strawberries that they probably picked that morning. Does Mom tell them that they must stay until all the strawberries are sold?

There's a mist in the air that makes everything seem dream-like. Hills and tree lines in the distance appear gray and unreal like a Monet Impression. When the road dips down, the mist turns to fog and I have to concentrate to see the road. It is 6:00 a.m. on a June morning and we are going to pick strawberries. Amish ladies take strawberry picking seriously. If I pick 16 quarts, I will consider it a "job well done!" They will pick up to 100 quarts.

I pick up three ladies at three locations. They come to the van each carrying a stack of much-used cardboard quart containers, so that they will not have to pay for new ones. How tall is a stack of 100 containers? They bring Whale of a Pail buckets and large Tupperware containers or boxes, as there is not enough room in the van for open quart containers. They will empty strawberries into larger, easier to manage containers. Usually one or two children accompany each lady. I wonder how many quarts I could pick if I had a helper or two.

The strawberry rows are long and seemingly endless. I start out bending over. After a while I change to kneeling, knowing that before it is all over I will be sitting in the damp dirt, straw, and squashed strawberries. The plants are still wet with dew and soon my hands, my jeans, and my shoes are wet. Somehow it seems right. This is strawberry picking—getting up early, before it gets too hot, wet hands, straw sticking to you, and the smell, "Mmmm!"

It is hard work, but well worth it. Listen to that sound! Is there any other sound like it? The snap/pop as you pull each strawberry off. "S-N-O-P!" I've invented a new word. It's half "snap" and half "pop."

"Snop! Snop! Snop!" as I pick, pick, pick.

It was almost cold when we began picking. "Snop!" Now it is almost hot. "Snop! Snop!"

I pick faster so I can finish. "Snop! Snop! Snop!" I stand up to stretch and a child several rows over smiles at me.

"I know her," I think. "Don't we drive her family?" Then her mother stands up and I do recognize her. It is the Rabers, and yes, we do drive them.

As I stretch I watch some other Amish children across the field. There seems to be as much looking and playing going on as there is strawberry picking. Like all Amish activities, this is an opportunity for the children to participate and learn some good work habits. At this point I would gladly take a child or two who only picks half the time and plays the other half.

I finish picking long before my Amish ladies do, as I pick so few compared to them. Even though I pick enough to freeze for a year of Strawberry Pancakes for the Bed & Breakfast, I'll finish with time to sit in the van and write this.

I remember one of the first times I picked strawberries with Amish ladies. When I was finished picking mine, I offered to help pick some for Rachel. There were other Amish ladies in the next few rows, so naturally they and Rachel began talking and naturally they were not talking in English. After a while I felt left out, so I told Rachel, "Unless you talk English, I'll stop picking strawberries!" She immediately went back to speaking English.

That was years ago, but it is still a joke between Rachel and me. Whenever she and her sisters talk in "Amish" and forget me, I have only to say, "I'll stop picking strawberries…" We laugh and then once again I am included in the conversation.

I have to stop writing now. The strawberry pickers are returning to the van, laden down with the fruit of their labor, quarts and quarts of strawberries. It will take a few more minutes to transfer strawberries from open quart containers to pails and buckets with lids that won't spill on the ride home. In the back of the van, under the seats, everywhere possible, strawberries are stacked. Still, some must be held on laps until we reach home.

We are hot, dirty, sticky, achy, and well ready to stop picking and start going home, but can you guess how good this van will smell all that way? Children in the back laugh and giggle in play, freed from working for a while.

"How many quarts did you pick?" I ask.

One answers, "75." Another says, "84." The last one says, "60." Let's see…with my 16 that makes 235 quarts of strawberries. No wonder the van smells so wonderful.

"I wonder what we will all be doing this afternoon," I say with a smile.

They all laugh, and answer, "Guess?" and "I wonder!" and "I have no idea!"

After a hard morning of picking, there will be no rest upon arriving home. Before these ladies go to bed tonight, there will be boxes and boxes of strawberries in assorted freezers, and you can know there will be strawberry pie for supper tonight. As I drive my strawberry-scented van home I have visions of Strawberry Shortcake, Strawberry Smoothies, and Katie's Strawberry Brownie Pizza.

Katie's Strawberry Brownie Pizza

1 brownie mix
8 oz. cream cheese (softened)
8 oz. Cool Whip
½ cup sugar
2 quarts strawberries (sliced)

2 Tbsp. clear jel
1 cup sugar
2 cups water
2 Tbsp. strawberry Jell-O

Mix brownie mix according to the package directions. Bake in 9"x13" pan. Cool. Mix cream cheese, Cool Whip, and ½ cup of sugar together. Spread on top of cooled brownies. Mix clear jel, 1 cup sugar, water, and Jell-O. Bring to boil and boil for 1 minute. Cool and add sliced strawberries to cooked mixture. Spread on top of Cool Whip mixture. Refrigerate for 2 hours.

Things that make me smile

A small Amish girl, with black head covering, violet-colored dress, and bare, dirty feet, on a hot summer day, picking and eating strawberries straight out of the garden.

The Little Milk Cow

For as long as I have known Deborah she has thought that having her own milk cow would make her life just perfect. The charm of milking it, tending to it, making her own butter, and having all that "free" milk was just what she thought she wanted. How quaint to look out her kitchen window while doing dishes and gaze upon her own milk cow grazing in the field across the lane.

Didn't her seven children need milk to grow strong and healthy? Hadn't they always had milk cows on this farm when she was growing up? There would be no more running out of milk at the worst possible time. No more hitching up the horse to the buggy, or riding her bicycle down to the small, local grocery store just to buy milk.

"Yes," Deborah thought to herself, "every Amish lady should have her own milk cow."

Not too long after that, her brother mentioned that he had this small cow which was a little hard to milk and he just didn't know if he was going to keep her. That was all Deborah needed to hear.

All her dreams of the charm of owning her own milk cow flashed before her eyes. This was her opportunity, there for the taking. Their farm and her brother's farm connected, so it was a simple matter of having her boys walk the cow to her barn. Almost as quickly as one could say the nursery rhyme where another cow jumped over the moon, she had her own little milk cow, and she had milk.

Almost from the first day her husband complained that the cow was indeed hard to milk, but being a good husband who wanted to please his wife, he milked the cow twice a day, and she had milk.

The children drank milk. All seven of them drank milk with every meal, and all seven of them drank milk with every snack, and she had milk.

Her husband still complained that the little cow was truly hard to milk, and that the cow kept trying to break out and run away, to return to the brother's farm, and did they really need all this milk, for she had milk.

Deborah made puddings and sauces, and cream soups, and cream pies, and custards, and still she had milk. She learned how to make butter although it was a little watery, it tasted fine, and all of the neighbors seemed to enjoy it, but still she had milk.

Her Amish, gas-powered refrigerator was just not as cold as the *Englich* electrical ones. It was an unusually hot summer, making the work for the refrigerator even harder. Gallons and gallons of warm milk, put warm into the refrigerator, just didn't cool quickly enough. Some started to spoil.

"Would the chickens drink milk?" she wondered. Gallons had to be thrown out, and still she had milk.

The children were getting tired of drinking so much milk. They asked if they couldn't have juice or lemonade sometimes. Deborah gave them more milk, and still she had milk.

Her husband picked at his dinner of steak with cream gravy, creamed corn, and mashed potatoes with lots of milk and butter, complaining that the little cow had gotten out again that morning, and was halfway back to her brother's farm before the boys caught up with her. Continuing his complaining, he reminded her that he didn't have time to chase cows, because it was time to get the hay in. Deborah quietly gave him a glass of milk, and still she had milk.

She gave milk to the neighbors, threw out some more that was spoiled, made cream of potato soup for lunch, and a huge caramel custard for dessert. She saw the back of the refrigerator for the first time in days, but still she had milk.

She learned to make yogurt, and mmmmm, was it good, and still she had milk.

Her sweet, patient husband got up early the next morning, mumbling under his breath as he headed for the barn to milk the little milk cow. It was already warm, and the fields of hay would not wait much longer. At the barn door, he saw an empty stall. The little milk cow had once again made an attempt to "return home."

In a not too patient voice, he called, "Boys, go find that cow, and take her back to your uncle! We've got hay to get in and no time to be chasing cows."

The boys soon found the little milk cow, and began to walk her "home." Halfway there, the little cow realized where they were headed, and took off at a trot, happily headed to the home she longed for.

In the kitchen it was discovered that all the milk from the day before had spoiled. Deborah walked outside to fetch that day's milk and found her husband hitching up the team, getting ready to go to the fields.

"Where's the milk?"

"There is none!"

"Why not?"

"The cow's gone back to your brother's. We just can't keep her here!"

"No cow?"

"No!"

"Well, did you milk her first?"

"No!"

"But…" and she had no milk.

As newborn babes, desire the sincere milk
of the word that ye may grow thereby.
I Peter 2:2

Things that make me smile

A cow that has stopped in the middle of the road. The Amish man who owns her alternates between pulling on a rope and slapping the cow on the rump. She had no immediate plans to move. My Amish passengers and I sit in the van laughing as tourists get out to take pictures.

July

"Knee high by the 4ᵗʰ of July."

That's the gauge farmers use to tell if their corn crop will be a good one or not. Knee high? The corn beside our Bed & Breakfast, which my daughter exclaimed over that morning in May, surprised by its sudden appearance, is now chest high!

Most years it reaches at least eight feet high, surrounding our B&B and seemingly placing us into our own little world. I love the privacy it affords, but miss the view of hills and fields and buggies coming down the road. I wonder how high it will grow this year.

I saw my first wheat shocks in a field today. Why does the sight of wheat or corn shocks always give me such joy? Perhaps it is because shocks are a part of the harvest, and what happier time of year is there than when the hard-worked-for harvest has become a reality. When, after all this time, a seed planted bears fruit.

Perhaps harvesttime reminds me to think: What spiritual seeds am I planting today? Love or Hate? Joy or Anger? Peace or Strife? Forgiveness or Resentment? When the harvest comes, what fruit will I bear?

I was late picking her up to go "garage sale-ing." When did "garage sale" become a verb? Was it about the same time that "greenhouse-ing" also became a verb? That's when we go from one greenhouse to another purchasing our plants for the garden, looking not only for the best bargain, but also for variety.

She hadn't noticed that I was late, as she had invited her sisters and a couple of nieces to go "garage sale-ing." One brought fruit pizza, one made blueberry turnovers, and another had baked cookies. With enough coffee, this constituted breakfast. They were too busy eating, visiting, and laughing when I arrived to even notice my tardiness. I was handed a plate of goodies and a to-go cup of coffee, and we were ready to hit the garage sales before the "greedy people" got there.

This is a long-standing joke that we have laughed about for far too long for it to still be funny, yet we continue to laugh. How does the joke go?

A certain woman was going to a garage sale *early* in the morning. Her husband asked her, "Why are you going so early?"

She replied, "The greedy people go real early to get the best bargains, so I want to get there ahead of the greedy people."

As usual, most of the fun is in being together, talking, visiting, sharing snacks, and laughing. There does also seem to be an element of, "Who gets the best bargain," or "Who buys the most," or best of all, "Who buys the largest item and therefore causes Joyanne the most grief as she tries to figure out how to get this item home."

People sit on each other's laps while items are stored under, behind, beside, and have even been tied on top of the van.

They seem to prefer garage sales put on by other Amish, but will go to any others along the way. With such large families, special attention is paid to looking for "plain" clothes that their children can wear. Once I questioned why they all walked past a rack of Amish ladies' dresses.

"Oh, those are too old-fashioned," I was told. So I think, but don't say, "Excuse me! Too old-fashioned!" Does anyone besides me see the irony in that statement?

Amish garage sales are often in unique places, such as, "Past the house, behind the barn, up a steep path." One I particularly remember was, "Past a pen with deer in it, past the house, behind the barn, between a hutch with four rabbits and a corral with two ponies."

Driving between sales, we talk, as women have talked for ages. We talk about our children, our household chores, what we have to do when we get home. Sometimes they talk about subjects I can't join into. The subject of their horses is one of them.

"Our horse scares easily, then goes to the middle of the road," Deborah says.

"Our horse doesn't scare easily, but he is slow," Ruth replies.

"Our horse is slow, too," Rachel says. "Sometimes Reuben gets impatient because he is so slow, but I like that he is slow and easier for me to handle."

The subject changes from horses to gardens, and from that to canning. While they compare how many jars of beans they have put up, I wonder why my bean plants didn't even come up this year. Deborah has put up 196 quarts of beans, but she is planning to use them for the wedding they are having in September.

Homemade cookies are passed around, and the subject changes again.

"Boy, it's getting hot out there!"

"Yeah, but it sure feels good in this van!"

I know it isn't just the weather or the temperature in the van that makes these outings seem so good. We have found a van full of bargains, we have eaten our fill of cookies and pretzels, we have had a day full of fun, laughter, visiting, and fellowship, but best of all, we *got there ahead of the greedy people.*

Things that make me smile

Laughter and chatter of sisters in the back of my van, enjoying each other so much because it has been months since all six of them were together.

Rachel's Fruit Pizza

Crust:

½ cup sugar

½ cup butter

1 egg

1⅓ cups flour

1 tsp. baking powder

¼ tsp. salt

½ cup milk

Topping:

8 oz. cream cheese

⅓ cup powdered sugar

1 Tbsp. lemon juice

2 cups whipped topping

Fruit Glaze:

2 cups pineapple juice

½ cup sugar

2 Tbsp. Clear Jel

  (or cornstarch)

Crust: *Cream together sugar, butter, and egg. Blend in flour, baking powder, and salt. Add milk, mixing well. Spread onto pizza pan. Bake at 350° for 10-12 minutes. Let cool.*

Topping: *Blend all ingredients and spread on cooled crust.*

Fruit Glaze: *Mix ingredients together; cook on low until clear and thickened. Cool. Add your favorite fruit to the glaze. (Peaches, apples, grapes, kiwi, strawberries, etc.) Spread on top of crust and topping.*

Seeing a Man about a Horse

I'm having trouble remembering the last time I drove Darius. Perhaps it is because of the time we went to see a man about a horse.

Over the phone he said, "I need to see a man about a horse." I almost laughed out loud when he said it, recalling that old saying, but I quickly stifled my mirth, realizing he was not joking, and being Amish, he had no idea that what he had said was funny. He truly wanted to see a man about a horse.

The first time I drove Darius I was mildly surprised at his unusually outgoing, jovial nature. Most Amish men that I drive are quiet and not very talkative. Darius always smiled, joked, and kidded with me.

He was a small, thin man, but his face had large features making him not unattractive, but certainly not handsome. He wore traditional Amish clothing, except the black straw hat he sported had been reshaped some, making it look more like a hat from the 1950s than the regular, flat-brimmed hats of the Amish. He wore it at a jaunty angle, which also surprised me. There was no beard, although he was probably in his mid thirties. He was unmarried. By tradition, Amish men do not begin to grow their beards until after they marry. Black-rimmed glasses completed the picture.

This last time I drove him he especially laughed and kidded me about my driving. The only vehicle available that afternoon was my husband's 4X4 truck which had a stick shift. I do know how to drive a stick shift, but don't drive this one often enough to do it with any smoothness. We jerked along, laughing and joking, until we reached our destination.

It was an average-sized house with a small barn, the size barn used by Amish who have chosen not to farm but still need a barn large enough to house a horse or two, a buggy, some hay, maybe a chicken or two, and of course some barn cats.

Darius got out, introduced himself to the man who was selling the horse, and went into the barn. I sat waiting in the truck, watching an Amish woman working in her vegetable garden, which stretched out beside the house. Though it was warm, and the afternoon sun was shining directly on her, she seemed unaffected by the heat and worked with a hoe, weeding neat, tidy rows of vegetables, removing weeds I was having trouble seeing because they were so small. In fact, I doubted any weed would dare grow in such a perfect garden.

It didn't take long before I was too hot to continue sitting in the truck, so I got out and walked toward the barn where there was some shade. Inside the barn it was surprisingly clean, but then it was a new structure with unfinished wood, yet unmarked, unrubbed, and unchewed by animals. For such a small structure, it had a high roofline with numerous small, square hay bales neatly stacked in its loft. Two small kittens peeked out from behind one bale. I longed to stroke them, but knew most barn cats are almost wild and would never allow me to touch them.

Darius and the man selling the horse were in a stall with a beautiful young horse. Shafts of light shone in on the horse's dark coat, showing reddish hues wherever the light hit. He seemed somewhat smaller than many horses. I commented on this. The men explained to me that he was a Morgan.

So that Darius could test drive him, the seller was hitching the horse to a buggy. This was probably the closest I had ever been to seeing a horse hitched to a buggy. From where I stood, it looked as if the seller was holding a hundred feet of leather straps and as many silver buckles. How could he ever know what went where? What buckle went to what strap? If you saw it done, how could you ever remember it? If someone dropped all that on the floor, wouldn't it become a useless pile of silver and leather?

"That looks so complicated. How do you remember where all that goes?" I asked.

"The same way you remember things on your car," the seller replied.

"How old were you when you learned it?"

The two men conferred. "About eight or nine," they agreed.

I probably stood with my mouth open!

Darius walked over to the horse's head. He held it in his hands and stood studying it. He commented on the size of the ears and the men explained to me that Morgan horses have smaller ears. He pointed out to the seller that, "His nose is a little crooked."

I don't know what came over me! Perhaps it was because of all the kidding about my driving that I had received on the way over. I usually don't mix in the business of the Amish I drive, but before I could stop myself I asked Darius, "Do you ever notice crooked noses and small ears on girls or do you only see them on horses?"

Darius turned five shades of red. The seller suddenly needed to study another part of the horse, and it obviously needed close studying, for he quickly buried his face around the horse's other side but not before I caught the laughter written all over his face. There followed some muffled spluttering sounds from that side of the horse, but the seller did not reappear for a few minutes.

Darius turned yet another shade of darker red, and answered me, "I'm not good with girls. Only horses," he stuttered.

He didn't buy that particular horse. I don't know if he bought another one, for as I said at the beginning of this story, I'm having trouble remembering the last time I drove Darius.

Be ye not as the horse… which has no understanding:
whose mouth must be held in with bit and bridle.

Psalm 32:9

Things that make me smile

Belgian horses, standing

tall and proud and strong,

with short cut-off tails; tails

that swish and twitch to

ward off flies, but somehow

seem to keep time to the

music on my van stereo.

August

Every Amish woman I know has run out of canning jars, including me. Oh, wait. I'm not Amish! You can't even buy them in stores. I know; I tried. Then I tried borrowing some. That's when I discovered that every Amish woman I know has run out of canning jars. Everyone's garden produced in abundance this year. Clay keeps coming in the door, a huge smile on his face, and with another bucket or bowl overflowing with garden bounty.

"Look at these tomatoes! And the plants are still blooming!" he beams.

I consider sneaking out tonight and pinching off a few blooms. He has been doing this for weeks! I have spent days freezing, canning, stewing, baking, and making jams and jellies.

I have given away tomatoes, sold tomatoes, canned tomatoes, and made chili, spaghetti, vegetable soup, and get this, *Tomato Muffins* for the Bed & Breakfast. They were actually quite good, *and* took five cups of tomatoes! Hooray!

Jars in a rainbow of colors line the shelves of my basement, as they must have done in this old farmhouse for over a hundred years. Is there any better sense of accomplishment or prettier sight to a country housewife than shelves full of jars displaying an array of summer colors? Green beans, red tomatoes, yellow corn, orange peaches, cinnamon apples, white pears (pink pears if I put a few raspberries in the jar), apple butter, pumpkin butter, and salsa with all the colors in one jar. They sit in neat rows, just waiting for us to enjoy them.

Does every country woman feel pleasure when she hears the "ping" of a jar sealing, letting her know that its bounty will be safe to eat long into the cold winter?

Canning is new to me. My mother never canned, so I taught myself with a book from the library. I had quite good results, but to spend the day in an Amish basement, canning peaches or applesauce, is so much more fun with a group than working by yourself. This is a lesson the Amish learned long ago and we *Englich* have somehow sadly forgotten.

With any gathering of Amish, they start early and bring food. As I am the Amish "sister" who drives, my first job is to pick up everyone. At each stop, children run out first, eager to begin a day of fun with their cousins. Their mothers follow, carrying some freshly made treat and tools to help with the canning.

As with the "Morning Coffees" the van soon fills with mouth-watering aromas. When we pull into Katie's driveway, children seem to appear from all directions—two from the barn, two from the house, and two more from the dog kennel. Eighteen-month-old Jeffrey spies the still-moving van and takes off, toddling as fast as his chubby little legs will go. Eight-year-old Michael grabs him before any harm can happen. I smile. How mature and loving for an eight-year-old, to take such good care of his younger brother!

We always eat, drink coffee, and visit first. The visiting can take an hour or two, but finally someone decides we must start the job at hand. Usually it is *Mommie* who says we must begin to work. If it's canning, it usually takes place in the second kitchen that most Amish homes have in the basement. This makes it cooler for summer canning, but I always remember the first time I sat down to peel apples in Ruth's basement kitchen and thought, "It's dark. Why don't we turn on a light?"

I usually sit and peel for hours, as that is one thing I know I can do. I bring my favorite knife, as do most of the others. (Is having a favorite knife an Amish trait?)

Someone gets the jars ready; someone else starts water boiling on the stove, while I peel. Soon there are enough peach slices for Carrie to begin putting them into the jars, thumping the jar on a towel on the table to make them settle into the jar.

Someone adds syrup. Flat lids and screw bands are put on by someone else, and jars are submerged in boiling water, while I peel.

After the right amount of time has passed, the jars are taken from the kettles, and set on the basement floor, which is spread with newspaper. Carrie has been filling and thumping jars all this time, syrup has been added, and lids put on, so that the next batch can be put into the kettles, and I am still peeling. The basement becomes warmer as the sun rises, and steam rises from the kettles. Children run in and out from their play, grabbing slices of peaches from the large bowls waiting to be put in jars. Isn't it good that "kid germs" don't count?

As I sit peeling I overhear *Mommie* say, "That jar is walking over."

"What does she mean?" I think to myself, seeing in my mind a jar that has sprouted arms and legs, and is walking across the floor. I know that makes no sense, but what else can she mean? Finally my curiosity overcomes me and I have to ask,

"What does she mean? How can a jar *walk*?"

Laughing, they explain to me that in "Amish," streams don't *run* they *walk*. So jars don't *run over*, they *walk over*. I tell them about my

vision of a jar with arms and legs, walking across the basement floor. We still laugh about that.

We break for lunch, and I get to stop peeling! Lunch will not last as long as breakfast, as finishing the job at hand can be clearly seen. With lunch over, some will tackle the dishes, while others go back to the task at hand, and I go back to peeling.

By mid-afternoon, the last jars will be in the kettle. Rows and rows of canned peaches line the floor, waiting for each lady to take home with her. They shine with golden goodness that seems to reflect our sense of accomplishment, and finally, I can stop peeling.

I heard Canada geese flying past this morning, for the first time this year. I ran to the window to watch them pass and listen to them honk. I hope I never tire of watching and listening to them.

There's a bit of mist hovering above the corn, along the creek, behind the barn early this morning. Could it be that autumn is coming? By noon, August's warm sun shines down on us, and on the many horses I see in the fields. Their coats are so shiny with health and youth that the sunlight reflects off their backs. By late afternoon it is so warm that the animals in the pastures seek shade under the few trees that are available. It's so warm that I feel an anticipation of autumn within me. Wasn't it just yesterday that we were so cold and tired of winter that we were longing for summer?

I'm seeing shocks of a crop, dotting the fields, I don't remember seeing before.

"What is that?" I ask Deborah, as we pass yet another field full of small shocks.

"It's oats," she answers me.

"Why don't I remember seeing this many shocks of oats, before?"

"Farmers weren't growing it, they were buying it. But lately it has been so expensive that farmers are growing their own. They feed it to the horses."

I look out to another field, off in the distance on a hill. How often have the different colors of fields reminded me of quilt blocks, sewn together with the stitches of fences? Now in some of the fields where the oat shocks stand, it looks as if some Amish lady has added the fancy stitches of **"French knots"** to her quilt.

Some Amish farmers are beginning to cut their field corn with equipment similar to that used by their forefathers. Perhaps it is the same equipment. The horses pull a machine, which cuts the corn, binds several stalks into a bundle, then drops it off the back onto the field. Someone will walk behind, picking up the bundles, placing them on a wagon or standing them up with other bundles in the field to make "shocks" which always remind me of Indian tepees. If they are put on the wagon, they will be taken to the barn and ground for silage.

When I pass Deborah's house I spy Darrel out in the field with *Daudi* (Grandfather). They are not harvesting corn, but with my limited farm knowledge, I cannot tell what they are doing. My interest lies in watching a grandfather sharing his knowledge and experience with the next generation. My next few minutes are spent watching *Daudi* show Darrel how to hold the reins, how to handle the horses, and where the farm equipment the horses are pulling should be. I pray that someday Darrel will know how blessed he is to have a grandfather who patiently instructs him. Youth, even Amish youth, don't always acknowledge the wisdom stored up within our elderly.

Oak Haven Summer Salsa

(Or what to do with all those extra tomatoes)

about 12 lbs. fresh, firm, ripe
    tomatoes (chopped) (Some
    people remove the skins; I do not)
2-3 medium to large onions
    (peeled & chopped)
4 or 5 diced bell peppers
    (green, red, yellow, orange)
1 cup apple cider vinegar

½ cup sugar
2 oz. salsa mix (Use half of a
    4 oz. package.)
    I use "Mrs. Wages" mixing
    a medium & a hot package
    together so it is not too hot
2-3 Tbsp. chili powder
    (optional)

Mix together, bring to boil, and simmer for one hour. (Cook longer if mixture has too much liquid and needs to evaporate some. Ladle into clean, hot jars. Process in boiling water for 40 minutes. Let stand for 12 hours. Check lids for seal. If not sealed, refrigerate. (Remember, this has no additives or preservatives, so it won't keep in the refrigerator as long as store-bought salsa.)

Things that make me smile

Big sister and little brother,

each on a swing, swinging

side by side in the beauty

of a warm summer

day, holding hands.

Hiram and the Deer

Every time I drive Hiram we see deer. Not every now and then. Not every other time. Every time!

The first time he pointed out deer, one group after another, I thought, "It must be just the perfect time of day when the deer come out to feed. So naturally we are seeing deer here, there, and it seems everywhere." But it happened again and again. No matter what time of day I was driving him, or where I was driving him, Hiram saw deer. In the field, next to the road, beside that stand of pines, way over there where they were hardly recognizable as deer, Hiram saw deer.

I asked him, "How do you see so many deer?" He just smiled.

A couple of times, after I had finished our Hauling and taken him home, I tried to look more intently for deer. I saw more than usual, but not as many as Hiram saw.

Hiram likes to hunt deer. He and his sons hunted often. I have to think that if you were going to hunt successfully, seeing deer would definitely help.

I thought long and hard about this. The deer are there. Even if I didn't see them, they are there. So why wasn't I seeing them? No, why *was* Hiram seeing them? Why was this such an enigma to me? Why did it matter to me?

All at once my mind was illuminated with a beautiful comparison. The Truths of God's Word, the secrets, are hidden throughout the Bible. They are there, even if I didn't see them. Many of us read the Bible without ever seeing those truths or secrets. Why?

"Seek and you shall find…" (Matt. 7:7).

You can't just glance at it, looking once then moving on to something more entertaining. Whether you are sighting deer or reading the Bible, you have to seek; you have to teach yourself to look, and look some more, even when you are tired of looking.

"If you continue in My Word…" (John 8:31).

Continue seeking and seeking until it becomes a habit. A more often used word would be PRACTICE. Hiram had practiced looking for deer until he could do it with very little effort.

How far could I take this lesson?

Practice *LOVE* until it becomes a habit.

Practice *PATIENCE* until it becomes a habit.

Practice *GIVING* and *FORGIVING* until it becomes a habit.

Practice *FAITH* until it becomes a way of life.

Practice *seeing God's beauty* everywhere I go instead of seeing my problems.

Practice *believing God's Word* until I believe it instead of my problems.

I may never be able to find deer as well as my Amish friend, Hiram, but I believe I am not only a better person, but also a happier person than I once was because of the lesson he taught me.

But whoso looketh into the perfect law of liberty, and
<u>continueth</u> therein, he being not a forgetful hearer…
this man shall be blessed in his deed.

James 1:25

Things that make me smile

Barefoot Amish children, running, laughing, playing in the front yards, totally enjoying life without the aid of any computerized toys.

September

September is starting out like
it is going to be a great autumn.
The mornings are cool, sweater weather, but the
afternoons are warm, and the nights are almost cold. Sleeping with an
open window means a light blanket is necessary, but what great sleeping
weather it is.

The corn is so high I can no longer touch its top with my
outstretched arm. How did it get so high in only a month? I have
become accustomed to the tall wall of corn that surrounds our
home and Bed & Breakfast. I know that any day now the harvester
and trucks will come and erase my privacy, cutting down in wide
swaths the wall I have so lovingly watched grow for all these months.
Though I will truly miss the corn, I am suddenly reminded of the
view I have missed and how my world will be open again and stretch
for mile upon beautiful mile.

Has autumn arrived? Only a tree here and there is beginning to
change color. For the most part, everything is still green. The roadside
stands are selling mums, pumpkins, cider, and all those things we

associate with autumn. They spill out from the stands almost to the edge of the road. I wonder how they can ever sell so many pumpkins.

Rachel has successfully raised "white pumpkins" with seeds from the white pumpkin I bought for her last autumn. She has promised me one for my autumn display, once they are a little bigger.

Our garden is almost spent. The potatoes are dug, the onions are hung, the green beans never did do much this year, the squash is all eaten, but the tomatoes keep coming.

Where is that recipe for Tomato Muffins that uses 5 cups of tomatoes? Is there such a thing as Tomato Jam? Yes! Here it is in the old *Kerr Canning Book.* Eleven cups of tomatoes! Yes, there is a God!

I've put up more applesauce, cinnamon apples, and apple butter than I thought was possible, and still we have apples on our trees. I know these are a kind of apple with a short shelf life, so rather than have them go bad, I'll share them with my Amish "sisters" by organizing a frolic.

What is a frolic? Like a barn raising, a frolic is when any group of Amish gets together to help someone with a job. It can be a barn raising, or house painting, or fence building, sewing, cleaning, or in this case putting up apples.

It is decided that we will all gather at Deborah's house, and naturally my first job is to pick everyone up in the van. As I begin to drive, I see yet another crop of hay being cut and stored. How many does that make for this year?

Are the leaves beginning to turn? Looking out at the trees I see just a hint of color every now and then. How long will it be until I see rust, orange, red, brown, and yellow?

Deborah has invited both sisters and sisters-in-law, so the basement is full, and the breakfast treats are many. I have brought Harvest Apple Cake. We eat and visit until *Mommie* once again reminds us that we must begin our work.

Bushel after bushel of apples are unloaded from the van, dumped into round, galvanized washtubs of water, and we all find our jobs and begin working. Can you guess what I do? How did you guess? I start peeling apples.

We are going to make apple pie filling. It will be put into quart jars and processed so that we can store apples for pies all winter long. It is decided that everyone will take home an apple pie (those with larger families will take home two), so some of the ladies go next door with *Mommie* to the *Daudi* house, and make pie after pie, while we continue to shred apples, mix ingredients, pack jars, and I peel apples.

Once again the basement grows warmer. Once again the children run in and out, grabbing apple halves, and once again we visit and talk and enjoy each other's company, hardly realizing we are working.

I remember the last time we all gathered to put up another abundance of apples that came from our trees. Esther, a sister-in-law, was just down the road, helping someone put up plums. On her way home, she noticed something going on at Ruth's house, pulled her horse and buggy over, and came into the basement to join us. After working all morning at another family member's house, she didn't hesitate for a minute, got out her knife and began peeling apples. When it was time for everyone to go home, I had to convince her that she should take some of the applesauce or apple pie filling. I could only talk her into taking enough apple pie filling to make one pie for that evening.

Esther probably won't remember this happening, as Amish work habits, ideas of sharing and doing and giving, are so ingrained into them that she would think this was truly "just the thing to do." I, however, am continually awed with their hardworking, unselfish, loving, caring way of life.

It was in September that our Amish family had a frolic to paint our barn. Somehow, with all we have to do, Clay and I had never gotten around to painting the barn, and did it ever need painting. Besides going years without paint, it was *white*. Everyone knows a barn should be *red*. If I am wrong, why is there a color called "barn red? Have you ever heard of the color "barn white"?

Every time we mentioned needing to paint the barn, Deborah's husband, Henry, would say, "Well, have a frolic. We'll get it painted." I had trouble believing he meant what he was saying. Why would anyone volunteer for so much work? So, I put it off for two more years. Finally, after he had said, "Have a frolic," several more times, I decided to take him at his word.

It took both of our vans to pick up everyone, early in the morning, the day of the frolic. They came, the men carrying tools, the women carrying food. Upon arriving at our home the men went right to work, as did the women.

Clay spent the day running to get tools from the basement, or driving to the lumberyard for additional supplies. I spent the day trying to find something for each woman to do every time she asked me, "What can I do now, Joyanne?"

Children, too numerous to count, ran and played, watched the men work, ran into the house to grab a cookie, and climbed trees that I suspect had never been climbed before.

One of the children had brought a puppy, which was lovingly carried around all day, being passed from one child to the next. At one point Emma Lou and Rebecca Joy wandered into the dining room, carrying the puppy, and discovered that I had Bed & Breakfast guests eating breakfast. The guests were enthralled with two Amish children and a puppy entertaining them at breakfast, even though at the time Rebecca could speak very little English, and Emma Lou had to translate for her.

The next time I turned around, I found Ruth pouring coffee for the guests, and making sure they had everything they needed. With her taking over that task, I could return to the kitchen and find work for the next few ladies who asked me, "What can I do now, Joyanne?"

The men continued working while we women prepared a turkey dinner for the lunch break. Every woman had brought a side dish to complement my turkey, gravy, and Southern Cornbread Dressing, so a huge meal was soon ready for eating. Children sat on the floor and outside. Men sat at the table, and women sat wherever they could find a place.

If we were at an Amish home, a silent grace would be said, but since we were at our home, Clay said grace out loud, in the normal *Englich* manner. Sometimes they ask Clay to say grace in their home instead of doing a silent grace, but the choice falls to the head of the household. If we are eating at the home of a grandchild, the grandchild leads us in silent prayer, while *Daudi* stands silent.

The lunch break was soon over, with every man eager to finish the tasks at hand. Many of them had chores at home to see to once they were finished here. We women had the usual job of putting away food, washing dishes, and cleaning up, but once again a mundane task was made fun with talk and laughter.

Our job was finished first, so we grabbed chairs and sat out on the grass, watching the men working and offering help and advice which was mostly laughed off and definitely ignored.

When the frolic was over, the barn had been primed and painted, an old rotten carport had been torn down, and the roof on an adjoining shed had been stripped of its old, leaking roof, and a new one had been put on in its place. We were all tired, but for me, it had been a fun, never-to-be-forgotten day. For my Amish family, it was just another day in the life of being Amish.

Harvest Apple Cake

1 cup vegetable oil
1 cup sugar
½ cup brown sugar
1 cup applesauce
3 eggs
3 cups flour
2 tsp. cinnamon

½ tsp. nutmeg
1 tsp. baking soda
½ tsp. salt
4 cups peeled, chopped apples
1 cup chopped walnuts or
   pecans
2 tsp. vanilla extract

In mixing bowl, combine oil, sugars, and applesauce. Add eggs one at a time, beating well each time. Combine dry ingredients and add to batter. Stir well. Fold in apples, nuts, and vanilla. Pour into a greased and floured 10" tube pan or Bundt cake pan. Bake at 325° for 1½ hours or until cake tests done. Cool in pan for 10 minutes before removing to cool on wire rack.

Caramel Icing
(May be drizzled on top)

½ cup packed brown sugar
¼ cup light cream
¼ cup butter

dash of salt
1 cup powdered sugar
chopped nuts (optional)

Heat brown sugar, cream, butter, and salt until sugar is dissolved. Cool to room temperature. Beat in powdered sugar until smooth. Drizzle over cake. Chopped nuts may be sprinkled on top if desired.

(One year when our pear trees had a tremendous harvest we substituted pears for apples with delicious results.)

The Wedding

If you ask an Amish person why most weddings are held on Thursday, in autumn, they will more than likely give you one of the two standard answers most often given by Amish to any question concerning their way of life:

1. "That's the way we've always done it."

2. "Tradition."

When asked how he could fit all of his large family into his buggy, Henry, Deborah's husband, answered, "Oh, they all fit, but when the knees of one child touch the knees of the child across from him, it's time to start marrying them off."

Amish weddings are an event! This event is planned and prepared for *months* in advance. First of all, the house, garden, yard, barn, shop, and any other surrounding buildings and property will be cleaned, straightened, repaired, and painted to as close to perfection as possible, for the wedding will take place at home. When Deborah's oldest daughter gets married, she will be the eighth one married on the family homestead. The actual wedding ceremony will take place in the barn. The reception will take place in the shop, which will have a rented tent added on to enlarge it.

A week before the wedding date, a "sisters' work day" has been called and all six sisters, and myself, will show up to clean, weed gardens, paint, or do whatever is needed. Naturally, my first job is to pick everyone up.

My first stop is Ruth's house. Just a short distance from her house I spot a group of children walking to school. I recognize the beautiful blond heads of Caleb, Josiah, and Rebecca Joy. It is Rebecca's first day of school. The excitement is clearly displayed all over her face. Because his older brothers and sisters are finished with school, for the first time, this year, Caleb is the oldest. It is now his responsibility to take care of his younger siblings, and his position of authority is also clearly obvious as he moves them down the road at a good pace. Caleb sees me first. A big smile breaks his serious face, and he waves at my van as it passes, at the same time moving the younger ones a little farther away from the edge of the road with a protective arm. The others recognize me and also wave. I never seem to tire of watching Amish children walking to school.

After the next two sisters are picked up, Lydia decides we must stop at Miller's Bakery and pick up some treats for breakfast. The van is soon full of the heavenly scent of fresh-baked goodies. Here we go again! No wonder I can't lose weight!

A short distance from Deborah's house we spot Henry, driving an empty wagon down the road. We all wave. He smiles and returns our waves. I later ask Deborah where he was going and she tells me he was on his way to help a neighbor with his hay. Even though he must have tons of his own work at home, with the upcoming wedding, he cheerfully rides off to help a neighbor. Could we learn from these people?

I drop off my load of sisters and children and head out for Winesburg where the youngest sister, Anna, lives, but before I go,

I grab one of the cinnamon buns from the Miller's Bakery box. I know it is too large for me, but saying I don't have time to go into the house, find a knife, and cut it in half, I take off, telling myself I will *only* eat half of it. It's a long drive to Winesburg, and when half of the cinnamon bun is gone and I find myself still nibbling on its sweet, warm goodness, I tell myself, "Stop eating, Joyanne!"

I don't hear myself!

When Anna and I get back to Deborah's house, there is a group of sisters standing around two wheelbarrows heaped high with corn, fresh from the garden. Obviously, the first job is going to be putting up corn. With so many hands making light work, the corn is quickly husked and taken into the basement. Kettles of boiling water await, as well as bowls, cutters to remove the corn from the cobs, and freezer bags.

After the corn is on its way to the freezer down the road, in a pony cart driven by Joel, Deborah's oldest boy, every window in the house gets washed, then we start cleaning the shop where tables and chairs will be set up for the reception.

In the afternoon, Rachel and I find ourselves without work for a few minutes, and decide to check out the barn where the service will take place. The men and boys have been cleaning it.

I have never been in such a clean barn. It smells of clean hay instead of the usual barn smells. All of the hay is neatly stacked on one side, all cobwebs have been removed by Darrel and Lavern, and the floor is swept clean, allowing us to see the *wide* boards that must have been here for over a hundred years. These wide boards had to have been cut from forests such as we can only dream about in our history books.

"There used to be a granary over there," Rachel said. "When we were kids we loved to play in the grain. Oh, to feel it under my feet again! Over here there was a swing. We had to jump to reach it." It is so easy to envision a "little girl Rachel" swinging in a dusty, dimly lit barn, dreaming "little Amish girl" dreams.

Together we walk over to the lower section of the barn, noticing wood grain, old, square head nails, and wooden pegs. We talk about when the barn was built. Rachel points out more things she remembers from her childhood. Indicating a wooden flue, she says, "This is where the grain came down from the granary above." Everything she points to looks as though it belongs in a museum.

We come upon Lab, Deborah's artistically named Labrador. Lab is curled up on a soft bed of straw with several kittens cuddled up next to her. Rachel points to where they used to keep the bull.

"I hated to feed the bull. He was loud and mean-looking. I was so scared of him!"

"What are you two doing in here?" Anna interrupts. "We're going to weed the garden. Don't you want to help?" Our trip down memory lane, in a historical barn, must come to an end. The garden needs weeding.

The Saturday before the wedding, because of Bed & Breakfast guests, it is late morning before Clay and I are able to arrive and see if we can help. The rented tent, which will extend the shop and allow a cooking area, is being set up. Women scurry everywhere, cleaning and setting up, but the men are erecting the tent. At each tent pole stands a man holding a rope, pulling it taut until Henry comes to them and secures the pole by tying the rope to a tent stake driven into the ground. In typical Amish fashion they wait patiently, holding their rope with no complaints.

Behind the tent, the rented kitchen trailer has been parked. How did they get that trailer up there in that tiny little space? I can't wait to check out this mobile kitchen on wheels. It has five stoves, three sinks, and more cabinets than I could ever dream of having in my own kitchen. Each cabinet contains dishes, pans, and utensils. Seemingly everything one could possibly need, and all with preparing huge quantities of food in mind, everything is carefully stored so not one inch of space is wasted. There are even dish towels, dishcloths, and pot holders. One whole end of the trailer, about 8'X10', is a walk-in refrigerator. Lined with refrigerator-style shelves, this will certainly be helpful to a household that customarily lacks adequate refrigerator space. The kitchen trailer is powered by its own generator.

I peek inside the shop. Usually a large empty room used for holding church services, and maybe a garage sale every now and then, it has been transformed into a reception area. The room is filled with row after row of tables and benches from the church wagons, enough to feed over 200 people. The tables are set with white tablecloths and dishes, silverware, sparkling glasses, and napkins in the color of the bride's choice. There is nylon net and ribbons along the length of each table with small candles placed periodically. At each place setting is a printed card with a song on it. The song will be sung by all before the dinner is begun. Then everything is covered with a cloth that keeps it all clean until the big day. Even with the covering cloth I can see how pretty each place setting is.

A Beautiful Life

(Tune: Life's Evening Sun)
This couple Lord, who now joined hands
Has hopes and dreams and future plans.
You are the one that knows the way
And that is why we humbly pray.

*Chorus
Lord be their guide, walk by their side
Till they with Thee forever abide.
Bless them with health and happiness
That reaches forth more souls to bless.

Oh may their life be full of love
A foretaste here of heaven above
That all the world in them can see,
The fullness of the trinity.

And with the clouds that hide the light
Dear Lord, make up a sunset bright
As they reflect on days gone by
A sunset fair will meet their eye.

The song card placed at each setting to be sung before dinner began.

In one corner is the *Eck,* appropriately named as the word literally translates, *"corner."* This is where the bridal couple will sit with what we *Englich* would call their "bridal party." The wall behind the *Eck* and the table itself have more decorations than other parts of the room. There is a wooden plaque with a marriage prayer on it, a Christian picture, a clock, and a shelf where flowers will be added later. Small, simple bouquets of flowers will be added to each table and the *Eck* will have a few extra flowers and the wedding cake. Everything shines beautifully in its simplicity.

The Monday before the wedding, the Bed & Breakfast keeps me busy until just before noon. By the time I arrive, hoping to help, everyone is eating lunch, and most of the work for the day is done. The ladies helping today are Henry's sisters and some neighbors. Even though I had done no work, I am invited to eat lunch. I have to fight feeling guilty. Not only have these ladies worked all morning, but they have also each contributed to this fabulous spread they are calling lunch. I have done neither, but it doesn't seem to matter to them. I am encouraged to eat.

Someone has brought a huge bowl of cookies. How many dozens does it contain? Every few minutes one of the children runs in from playing outside, grabs a cookie, and runs back out. What a childhood!

After lunch I get to help cut up some celery for the dressing. Even though one or two ladies could easily do the job in about an hour, with six of us it is done in a few minutes. Amish women don't stand and watch. They grab a knife, or whatever tool is needed, and join in the work. This is one habit I am glad I have learned from them.

Then I help mix the spices into the coating for the chicken. Our bride has some definite ideas how this coating is going to taste, so we spend quite some time mixing large bowls over and over as she adds this, then that.

Later that day, after nearly everyone had left to go home and begin cooking dinner for her family, I find a "wedding book" on the kitchen table. The wedding book belonged to the bride's cousin, and was being used as a guide to help Deborah. When the wedding is over, our bride will have her own wedding book, a reminder of all the people who helped to make this a special day. Once again I am awed at the organization it takes to plan an Amish event.

Listed on one page of the book are the following titles:

Eck Servers, Parent Table, Wedding Coordinators, Water Servers, Coffee Servers, Guest Book (young people responsible for seeing that everyone signs the guest book), Dishwashers (I wonder how you get picked for this job), Gift Receivers (young boys who greet each guest as they arrive, take the gifts from them and place them in the designated place for gifts), Baby-sitters (usually preteen girls, not yet old enough to serve at the tables), and Hostlers (usually four older boys who can carry water, empty trash, help with the horses, and carry any kettle of food too large for the women). Beneath each title were listed the names of family members, friends, or neighbors who were chosen for this position.

Another page is titled "Cooks" and under it, subtitles of Dressing, Vegetables, Potatoes, etc. Here again, names were listed of those who were chosen for these duties. These ladies will arrive however early enough it takes to cook and have the food prepared for the reception.

Sister-in law Susie told me she doesn't mind coming at 5:30 a.m. to fry the chicken, because then she will have the rest of the day free to enjoy the wedding. Maybe that works for her, but I would be so tired from getting up that early that I could hardly enjoy the rest of the wedding. Guess I'm not as Amish as I thought I was.

Further in the wedding book I find detailed instructions for each food item with each cook or helper listed on the page. I was later to find out that these pages would be posted in the kitchens, the basement, *Mommie's* house, or wherever the task must be performed so everyone would know where she was to work and how she was to do it.

Tuesday before the wedding is the day picked for Deborah's sisters, aunts, and other relatives to help. Yesterday, they toasted bread, cooked potatoes and carrots for fried dressing, and also mixed the salad dressing and put it in bottles. Today's list includes Clay driving Henry to get the chicken, bake pizza crusts for fruit pizza, cook fruit pizza filling, peel peaches, put green beans in kettles, and cut ham for beans.

Just as I'm thinking I can leave and go home, the bride and her cousin, Rosemary, approach me and ask if I can take them to buy some more flowers. The flowers the bride grew for her own wedding, starting in June, have not proven to be enough, so we jump in the van and take off to buy some more. When we return with the flowers, many hands make light work of unwrapping, trimming, and arranging the flowers. It is the end of a pleasant, busy, yet productive day, as we stand under the rented tent, completing this task. We are one day closer to the wedding.

On Wednesday we peel potatoes. How long does it take to peel 250 pounds of potatoes? I don't know! I lost track of time! The dressing is put together. This involves a dozen large bowls being placed on a table with the recipe where everyone can see it. Five of us share this job. One person goes around the table measuring into each bowl the first ingredient listed. The second person follows, adding the second ingredient, and so on, with another person going from one bowl to another, stirring and stirring and stirring. When all ingredients have been added, some discussion takes place. "Yes, *I* put in the salt." The dressing is ready to be put in storage containers until tomorrow when it will be fried.

Deborah has decided that she does not want her sisters cooking chicken on the day of the wedding, so the chicken will be cut up and cooked today. As well, topping for the fruit pizza will be made, pineapple cut up, blueberries thawed, and tea made.

The day of the wedding, my job starts at 6:30 a.m. I am to pick up Mary Ann. In an *Englich* wedding, Mary Ann would probably be considered the Maid of Honor or Bridesmaid. In an Amish wedding, the bride chooses her best friend, sister, or cousin, and the groom chooses his best friend, brother, or cousin. They in turn ask someone to join them, so that two couples stand with the bride and groom during the church service, and sit on either side of them at the *Eck*. They are called Witnesses.

Mary Ann is ready, dressed in an identical dress to the bride—navy blue with a white apron and cape. We talk a little about the weather; how it will be for the wedding. The sky is mysterious, not giving us any hints of the day ahead.

Close to Deborah and Henry's house we pass a woman walking along the side of the road. She has on a coat against the still cool morning, but showing below her coat I plainly see a white apron. Undoubtedly, this is a neighbor, making her way to the wedding to help with preparations.

Henry and Deborah's home is a beehive of activity. In every kitchen, women are working. The entire basement is an assembly line of women and food. Outside, behind *Mommie's* house, beside the shop, in an out of the way back corner, I find some older ladies frying the dressing. I don't recognize any of them. Are they neighbors or church members?

"Why are you ladies back here? Have they stuck you back here because you are known to misbehave?" I ask with a big smile.

No actress in Hollywood could have put on a more innocent face, as one of the ladies smiled and answered me, "Oh, we don't know how to misbehave!"

I have no other set job this morning, so I wander from one workstation to another, greeting those I know, explaining who I am to those I don't know. I offer to help, but everyone seems to have his or her task well in hand.

Because the service will be three hours long, and in a language we *Englich* do not understand, the Amish are kind enough to allow us

Englichers to only have to sit on the backless, hard wooden benches for the last hour of the wedding. I wander into the lower section of the barn, where I find 41 horses tied up or in stalls. Across the road, where the buggies are parked, are more horses tethered by rope, as there is only so much room in the barn.

I wander by the gift table and smile at the assortment of unusual gifts placed there by the gift receivers, and I smile, remembering how seriously those young boys went about their task this morning, practically grabbing gifts from some guests, being so intent to do their job. There was no "gift registry" or chosen "china pattern," so there will be no overly priced china or place settings that might never be used. The array of gifts is practical, thoughtful, and many are not wrapped, as in some cases that would be impractical. How do you wrap a mailbox, a barbecue grill, a wheelbarrow, or a weed eater? How much nicer the rake, shovel, and hoe look unwrapped with a large red bow around them. There's a cooker for canning and a stepstool. Also not wrapped are a garden hose, a bucket filled with cleaning supplies, and another bucket filled with small garden tools. A couple of gifts are wrapped using a new towel instead of wrapping paper. The bow is made of a matching washcloth. Many gifts are wrapped and will be opened later, after everyone has eaten. Then we'll see many more helpful items that this couple will need to start a new life.

I can guess, from attending other weddings, that there will be an iron and ironing board, dish drainer, bowls, towels, canning jars, perhaps a lantern or some tools for the groom, and always a coffee server to keep coffee warm. For without electricity, coffee gets cold quickly once the gas stove is turned off. Hopefully there will be a popcorn popper and maybe an ice cream bucket.

Soon I am drawn into the wedding service and slip into a back row seat where Clay is already seated. Though I can't understand much of what is being said, I am pulled into the atmosphere. After all, it is a wedding, and I am a woman.

The barn seems even cleaner than the day Rachel and I walked through it. One whole wall is hay, stacked from floor to ceiling. Pigeons roost on beams above us. (Is that safe?) There's a window open high up on the wall, where I didn't even realize that there was a window. No stained glass window is needed here. Through the window I can see a picture-perfect view of God's creation—rolling hills, green fields, and trees of every color. The view seems bright against the dimness of the barn's interior.

Though there are flowers on the tables set for the reception, and on the *Eck,* the bride carries no bouquet, and the only decoration in the barn is one hanging basket of petunias. Its lone beauty seems amplified by its ordinary surroundings.

We *Englich* sit in a section across from the main seating area. Rows of benches face rows of benches with the ministers in the middle. The bridal party sits in the front row. A sea of faces is spread in front of my view, so many I know, so many I don't know, all seriously listening to the message. I will always remember the bride in the first Amish wedding I attended. Dorcas was always cheerful, laughing, and smiling. Yet here, for her wedding, what most *Englich* say is the happiest day of a girl's life, she was solemn, without a smile anywhere in sight, *and* she had on a *black* head covering instead of the normal, pristine, pure white covering I have grown to love seeing on Amish women. I was so happy to see, that as soon as the service was over, she changed to a white head covering and was her usual smiling, happy self. When I asked a friend about this later, she explained that the wedding service was a serious matter and not to be taken lightly.

In front of me, our bride, in her hand-sewn navy blue dress with the white apron and cape, her face pure and unadorned as God made it, is to me more beautiful than those I am used to seeing who may spend thousands of dollars on a gown, and then more money to get their hair and makeup done professionally.

We *Englich* sit for our time in the service, catching a word every now and then that I could translate, but mostly just watching. I notice a collection of men's hats all piled on a beam out of the way. How will they know whose is whose?

Some smaller children become restless and are taken out, or move from Mom's lap to cross over to the men's side of the church to sit on Dad's lap. Groups come and go, each in their matching colors; table servers wearing different shades of blue and green, cooks wearing dark blue, and babysitters wearing sky blue. They come and go as time from their duties allows, catching a part of the ceremony. They slip quietly into the back section, designated for them and for us *Englich*.

Then in the midst of three hours of a language we cannot understand, suddenly our wandering minds are sharply pulled back to the minister as he says five words in English. "Divorce is not an option!"

Did God have someone *Englich* in mind with those five words? I look around sheepishly. Surely it must be one of those other *Englich* couples and not Clay and me.

Finally the bride and groom stand and take their vows. There is no "kiss your bride" or clapping from the congregation after the vows are said. They are married, nonetheless, and my heart swells with joy to witness this child I have known since she was 12 years old become such a beautiful bride.

There will be no photographer taking an inordinate length of time to take photos, so the reception meal is served almost immediately. We are seated at the *Englich* table. What a feast awaits us. Salad, chicken, dressing, potatoes, gravy, rolls with butter, two kinds of dessert, and ice cream are all served by young girls who seem to glide through spaces that don't seem wide enough for them to walk through, as time after time they pass steaming bowls of food, coffee, tea, and water. I must profess that everything is delicious, even if I did help prepare some of it.

When we can eat no more, we wander out to spend a pleasant day visiting and just enjoying the relaxation and company of each other. Groups of servers and helpers, finished with their work, pass here and there, visiting, a wave of pleasant color as they pass, all dressed alike.

The bridal party opens gifts while some of us sit and watch. Among the many gifts, there are three popcorn poppers. *Mommie* is overheard whispering, "I hope they like popcorn."

Children run and play and invent games to entertain themselves. Candy has been passed out to the children and soon the ground is littered with candy wrappers. Some of the children have found out where the ice cream is stored, and they make one trip after another to the freezer, helping themselves.

Emma Lou is feeling all grown up and excited because she is wearing a *cape* for this wedding instead of the "little girl apron" her younger sister Melissa is wearing. The apron is what my 92-year-old mother would call a "pinafore," a sleeveless, shift-style garment, made of matching material to the dress, worn on top of the dress to keep the dress clean.

Clay makes a late-afternoon trip in the van, as some of the brothers have cows that must be milked. Soon they return and begin to think about food again. How can they think about eating already? There is now food set out in cafeteria style and anyone can help themselves.

Young people arrive—young people related to the bride and groom, friends, neighbors, or church members. They will be fed a meal as we were fed earlier in the day. The bridal party, again seated at the *Eck,* is served a different meal. At this time the cake is cut, with no ceremony, and no help from the bride and groom. Most of it is put in boxes to be taken home by guests.

Women have been cooking, serving, waiting tables, washing dishes, and keeping this "wedding machine" going all day. They still smile and visit with one another, seemingly happy in their work. Others of us join them, washing dishes, cleaning up, putting food away, and beginning to put items back into the kitchen trailer.

When the young people have finished eating, tables are stripped, more dishes are washed, and before I know what is happening, suddenly men have joined the workforce and benches are being folded up to put in the church wagons, tables are folded up, and floors are swept.

While searching for some missing silverware, I find the same activities going on in Deborah's kitchen, her basement, and *Mommie's* house. No one issued the order, "Clean up!" It just began. It is the Amish way of life, and it works!

There is no honeymoon for an Amish wedding couple. In fact, they help with the cleanup, and will spend their wedding night at the home of the bride's parents.

The next day will bring more work—taking down tents, restoring the barn to a barn, and moving gifts to their new home. There they will begin their new life together; a life surrounded by a loving family, steeped in traditions that have survived hundreds of years, and is rooted and grounded in God's ways.[1]

Now the Lord God said, It is not good (sufficient, satisfactory) that the man should be alone: I will make him a helper meet (suitable, adapted, completing) for him... Then Adam said, This (creature) is now bone of my bones and flesh of my flesh. She shall be called Woman because she was taken out of man. Therefore a man shall leave his father and his mother and shall become united and cleave to his wife, and they shall become one flesh.

Genesis 2:18, 23 & 24 (Amplified)

---

1 Deborah's oldest two daughters were married within 10 months of each other. "The Wedding" is actually a combination account of both weddings.

Things that make me smile

Corn shocks standing tall in the fields, placed there by hardworking hands, toiling together as a family, or helping out a neighbor; whatever it takes to bring in the harvest.

October

$\mathbf{I}$s there a special kind of sunlight that comes only with autumn? As I sat at my desk working one evening, I paused for a second to look out the window. The cornfield in front of me became suddenly alive with **golden light** as the sun sets. My work had to wait as I stared in wonder. Then just as suddenly, the **golden light** was gone; only to be enjoyed for a brief time. Had I not looked up at that precise moment, I would have missed an awesome sight.

Did Someone make me look up? It had been an extremely long, hard, frustrating day, and then the **golden light** was there, as if to say, "I'm still here, Child."

"Thank you, Lord."

I've awaited the colors of autumn with the enthusiasm of a child awaiting Christmas. Is it later this year? I've seen only a spot of color here, another there—red, gold, and burgundy.

The other day, as the sisters and I drove to Canton, we marveled at how much more color there was, just those few miles north of home. Yesterday, I was finally seeing whole trees of color. Rust brown, lemon yellow, and peachy colors finally please my impatient eyes. Today the autumn sky is a perfect blue background to the maple tree in my front yard as I drive past for another Hauling.

Colors always seem vibrant, bolder, and more vivid in autumn. Everywhere I look there is a picture-perfect scene, worthy of a photograph. Burgundy leaves against an autumn blue sky. Pumpkins sitting beside a mailbox are bright orange with purple mums next to them. I would never have thought to put those two colors together, yet they are wonderfully pleasing to the eye. Bright yellow daisies, still blooming from the summer, mix easily with all this autumn pleasure. Gourds and squash in every shade of green and yellow, with shapes that are not to be believed, and ears of Indian corn add even more color to displays.

A sign over there says, "Pumpkins—Pick your own," and points to a field *full* of pumpkins of every size and shape, from tiny to huge, and in every shade of orange imaginable.

Apples, apples, everywhere apples—red apples, green apples, yellow apples, and what goes better with autumn than apple butter? Have you ever had apple butter that was made in a huge cast-iron kettle, over an open fire, which takes all day to make? I'm not sure which is more fun, taking turns stirring or eating the finished product. *Mommie*'s sister remembers their mother saying, "I could live off of bread with apple butter and coffee."

Some Old Order Amish have harvesting machines that remove the corn from its stalk in the field. It is fascinating to watch the horses slowly pull this machine through row after row of corn, while gleaming cobs of golden harvest shoot out the back, to be caught in a wagon. When the wagon is full, it looks like a wagon load of yellow gold, traveling down the road, contributing to our riot of autumn colors.

Fun scarecrows are set out with corn shocks and mums of every color from white to burgundy. Ah, the chrysanthemums! God's last splash of color just before the darker, gray and white, colorless days of winter set in. It's as if He is making a promise with their delightful little bursts of color: "I'll be back in the spring, with more color, more flowers, more life."

Autumn at Oak Haven Bed & Breakfast is a time to harvest friendships. It is our busiest time of year, and the time when many of our return guests, now friends, come back to visit. It is a time to sit on the porch, sip warm apple cider, perhaps have a slice of pumpkin bread, visit, share, and catch up on our lives. They always want to know how our Amish family is doing.

"You should have seen Deborah's boys the other day," I tell them. "They found an old goat cart in the back of the barn, dragged it out, and were giving each other rides in it, taking turns being the goat or the passenger. Just a little bit later one of them found a small 'caution/ orange triangle' such as are usually seen on the back of buggies. All riding had to stop long enough for one of the boys to attach it to the goat cart, then off they went again, having fun."

"And how is your mom doing?" guests also often ask.

"Oh, you've got to hear this story. The other day the Senior Citizens van came to pick Mom up. As Don, the driver, was helping Mom to her seat, they could hear laughter all throughout the van. One of the other passengers said, 'Don, you've got an extra passenger.' Don turned around to see that one of our chickens had boarded the van and was walking down the aisle, looking back and forth as if she was trying to decide which seat she wanted to sit in."

I finished by explaining, "She is one of our older chickens. Perhaps she thinks she is a Senior Chicken."

And before we know it, it seems as if autumn is gone. Was it shorter than usual, or was I just so busy this year? We did manage to drive around on a few Sunday afternoons and were not disappointed. Though there were not the wide expanses of colors we have grown accustomed to, there were splashes of color here, there, and over there.

"Oh! Look over there!" we would point and exclaim over and over.

There was this one spot, alive with autumn color, on the way back from the village, that caught my eye, but sadly I was in a hurry. The next time I was driving back from the village it was getting dark, so I could not see what I had only caught a glimpse of days before. As the old saying goes, "You have to take time to smell the roses," or in this case, enjoy the autumn colors. So I put forth the effort, no matter how busy I was, to drive to the spot, park, and just enjoy.

There, in the small patch of only ten to twelve trees, was *every* color autumn had to offer. The trees shimmered slightly in the cool evening breeze as if to accentuate their beauty. I sat and enjoyed God's glory until darkness overcame the area, then I drove home refreshed, more at peace, and with my soul somehow feeling as if it had been fed.

Oak Haven B&B's Pumpkin Bread

Sift together:
3½ cups flour
2 tsp. baking soda
1 tsp. baking powder
2 cups sugar
1 Tbsp. cinnamon
½ tsp. cloves
½ tsp. nutmeg
½ tsp. salt

Cream together:
4 eggs
⅔ cup water
1 cup oil (or applesauce may
    be used for part of the oil)
2 cups cooked and pureed
    pumpkin
1 cup nuts or raisins
    (optional)

Mix all ingredients together. Pour into greased loaf pans. Bake at 325° for 1 hour. Test with toothpick.

(This recipe is one of my favorites as it uses 2 cups of pumpkin. We always have ample amounts of pumpkin at Oak Haven, as we use so many to decorate each autumn and can't bear to just throw them away after Thanksgiving.)

Visiting Amish Schools

Respect, Honesty, and Responsibility. How often do you see or hear those words in our schools today? Yesterday I saw those words on a sign hanging on the wall of an Amish schoolhouse. That was just the beginning of what I was privileged to witness while visiting seven Amish schools with six eighth grade students and two teachers. I came away awed at the sights I had seen, yet almost in tears for what has happened to our American schools.

Nearly all Amish schools are entered by the basement. There, in the basement, you will find hooks on which to hang coats or sweaters and shelves for hats, bonnets, lunch boxes, and gloves or mittens. In one school there were baseball gloves on all the shelves. That school, I was told, was going to visit a neighboring school later in the day and play baseball. In another school I saw small metal cups hanging around a sink. Each cup was hung on a hook, which had a name tag.

Most Amish schools are old. Some are actually our own, abandoned public, one-room, country schoolhouses, which the Amish have bought for their use. They actually have school bells, hanging like church bells in small steeples above the roof. I asked if the bells are still used. "We ring them when recess is over," the teacher answered.

The desks and other furniture are also mostly old; older in some schools than others. In three of the schools that we visited they had the old type desks where the bench for the seat in front of you is actually part of the desk you are using. These were fastened together at the bottom on boards, in groups of three. I guess this keeps you from pulling out the seat of the student in front of you.

Many of the desks had small trash bags attached to the side of each desk with the aid of a magnet/clip. I had noticed that there was no central pencil sharpener run by battery or even a hand-cranked version. Each child had their own handheld, plastic pencil sharpener. Until I noticed the individual trash bags I had wondered where they would put their pencil shavings.

Only one school that we visited had indoor plumbing. The rest had outhouses, usually "Boys" on one side of the schoolyard and "Girls" on the other side. One of the girls on our visiting tour pointed out one set of outhouses, which only had "G" and "B" on them. She let us know that the "G" meant that was the "GOOD" outhouse, and the "B" was the "BAD" outhouse. I took advantage of that one school with indoor plumbing while I had the chance.

While trying to find one school, we passed some children walking along the road. Two girls came to a place next to a field and went through the fence. One girl held up the wire while the other went through, then they reversed and the one that was through held up the wire. As we were having trouble finding this school, I asked our teacher, "Do we have to go through that fence to get there?" A little farther down the road we found a lane that led to the school we were searching for and no one had to hold the wire up high enough to let the van through.

We entered the first school to the sound of children singing. It was difficult for me to understand their words, for Amish school children sing in a chanting fashion. They stood at the front of the classroom, to welcome us with their singing.

All the schools we went to had benches at the back or side of the classrooms for visitors to sit upon and observe. This first school was a new building. When it becomes necessary to build another school, it will be done in Amish, "barn raising" fashion. All those whose children will attend, as well as neighbors and family, will contribute, and a school gets built with no government aid.

Children do daily cleanups around the school, but when a major cleaning needs doing, or painting is required, families of students will see to it that the job gets done. In schools that are heated with wood, each family supplies a load of wood when it is their turn. The families of those children attending pay for the entire expense of the school. Again, no government aid is used.

This new school was bright and airy, with many windows. Even on a dull day, with no electric lights, it would be a bright room. Yes, one room for eight grades. Sometimes there is a curtain that can be pulled down the middle to divide the room.

There were bright signs hung on the walls, similar teaching aids that you would find in any classroom. However, most of these would not be allowed in our schools anymore.

In every classroom there was Easter art done by the children. There were no Easter eggs or Easter bunnies with baskets. Instead there were crosses which said, *"He is risen,"* and brightly colored flowers, some saying, *"Spring is here. He is risen,"* and others saying, *"Lo, the winter is past…"* "What verse of scripture is that?"

From one ceiling hung a sign which said, *"A face without a smile is like a lantern without a light."* I thought the use of a lantern was so appropriate for an Amish child. On the opposite side of this hanging sign it said, *"The best way to get even is to forgive."*

In two schools I saw a poster reading, *"If you don't have time to do it right, you don't have time to do it again."* What wonderful lessons to plant into young minds when those minds are at the best time to absorb and retain information.

One class had displayed their pictures of Noah's Ark, with dozens of animals stuck on them. Can't you remember the fun of playing with two of everything in Noah's Ark?

In two other schools there were posters proclaiming the "Fruit of the Spirit: Love, Joy, Peace, Kindness, Goodness, Patience, Gentleness, Faithfulness, and Self-Control (Gal. 5:22 & 23) Can we ever have too much of those?

I liked the bulletin board in one school, which had footprints all over it. Across the top was written, "Footsteps to Good Values," and on each footprint was a word: sharing, kindness, responsibility, honesty, patience, respect, and obedience.

On the blackboard of one school, and yes, it was a <u>black</u> board, was written, *"What belongs to you, but other people use it more than you do?"* I am still trying to figure that one out!

Five out of seven schools displayed the Golden Rule in a prominent place. Twice it was carved into wood, *"Do unto others as you would have them do unto you."* As if to sum it all up, in one school the banner in front simply said, *"God is Love!"*

In 1972, the Supreme Court Case of Wisconsin vs. Yoder decided that Amish should be allowed to educate their own children, and only educate them through the eighth grade. Most Amish schools have two teachers, usually one for the lower grades and one for the upper grades. They are usually unmarried girls who have only been educated through the eighth grade themselves.

One of the schools we visited had a young male teacher. He was outgoing and enthusiastic, and I thought infinitely patient as I observed him explaining how to check the answers on long division problems.

At the front of each classroom, usually beside the teacher's desk, is a long table. This is used when the teacher calls up each individual grade. She will announce something like, "First graders, come up front and bring your arithmetic books." She will then give instructions to the other grades that will keep them busy while she is teaching the first graders.

In the seven schools we visited I watched as every student sat quietly reading, doing arithmetic problems, or studying some lesson while their teacher's attention was on the group of children at the front of the classroom. Not once did any of these children cause a disruption, make a loud noise, get out of line, or in any way interrupt his fellow classmates. If one of them had a question, they waited until the teacher was between groups, and then raised their hand to indicate that they needed help.

Before any lessons were done, as each child was called up front for the first time of the day, he or she was asked to recite their memory verse to the teacher. *"...I will never leave you or forsake you...Hebrews 13:5,"* the little first grade girl recited. Her little classmate needed help with his memory verse, so the teacher quoted it aloud with him. I was told that they have a new memory verse each week.

The arithmetic lesson was then taught. Instructions were given for these children to work on after they returned to their desks. "Are there any questions?" she asked them. "Then you are dismissed. Second grade, you may come up with your arithmetic books." And so it went, group after group, grade after grade, subject after subject, sometimes to five or six children, sometimes to only one child.

The third school we went to was different in that one teacher had only three special education students, and the other teacher had grades one through seven. On the wall to the left of where I sat I saw some students' artwork showing their names and grades. There were three in first grade, one in second grade, one in third grade, two in fourth grade, two in fifth grade, one in sixth grade, and two in seventh grade. I realize that this was only twelve students, but she was teaching *seven* grades.

She glided around the room helping this child, instructing that one, calling the first graders up to the front for arithmetic, and then answering a question for another child.

How did she change back and forth from one grade to another, from one subject to another, from one child to another? I'm surprised I didn't swallow a fly, for I know my mouth must have hung open watching her teach. Imagining myself in that position, I could only see chaos.

"What is your name? What subject are you studying? What grade are you in? Third? Weren't you in second just last year?"

Using flash cards with the first graders, they called their answers aloud to her, eager to be the first to call out the correct answer. There was some sort of game being played, the rules of which I did not know, but the attitude of these children to learn was contagious.

When we got back to the van, I asked one of the teachers how the special education students would be taught.

"They will be taught at the level they can handle," she answered.

I asked her how she would teach a child with dyslexia, wondering if she would even know what dyslexia was.

Without hesitation she answered, "A dyslexic child would require more one on one time." I liked her answers.

In most of the schools, the children introduced themselves. The teacher would call them up by family name, as in "Jacob & Martha Miller." The children of this family would go to the front of the class, arrange themselves in numerical order, oldest to youngest, and then tell us their name, their grade level, and possibly their favorite subject. Some of the older ones looked typically, adolescent bored, while some of the youngest seemed shy and could hardly be heard.

As a special welcome to us visitors, at most of the schools the children sang to us. Sometimes they were called to stand up front. They seemed to know where to stand without any instruction. Other times half of the class moved over to the other side of the room, and slipped in beside a fellow student to share their desk or chair. Again no instruction was necessary, and each child was seated quickly and quietly with no fuss. I did notice that boys shared chairs with boys and girls shared chairs with girls. Wouldn't you expect some shoving or resentment as in, "This is my chair! Move over some!" There was none.

The songs they sang were a delight to hear, not just because children were singing, but because of the words. I wrote frantically, trying to get down some words, but was only able to get this much.

"Why complain about your clothes or shoes?"

"Be thankful for the good things that you've got."

"Why complain about the way you look?"

"Why complain about the scolding you took?"

"The good things that you've got, for many are just a dream…"

In another school they sang about the little boy whose loaves and fishes Jesus used to feed the five thousand.

"…Add a little faith, subtract all your doubt, it's sure to work out."

"I can tell by the smile and the twinkle in your eye, the Master's taught you how to multiply."

"…Add a little faith, subtract all your doubt, watch it all work out."

I wanted to clap! One doesn't clap in an Amish school, for the sake of not promoting pride, but when they finished, I was so overcome, *I wanted to clap!*

My daughter, who teaches in our public school system, tells me she sees fighting, unhappiness, and disobedience every day. She was allowed to visit an Amish school a short while back and as she put it, "I was touched by how happy those children were. They seemed at peace and filled with a simple joy that is, sadly, hard to find in our public schools."

To have spent the day observing precious children being taught in a godly, constructive, pleasant, uplifting environment was overwhelming. There is a new task ahead of me. I will be praying for our schools, that our children may be educated as Amish children are educated. Please join me!

Train up a child in the way he should go: and when
he is old, he will not depart from it.

Proverbs 22:6

A Pupil's Alphabet

(Posted on the wall of Buckeye School, Farmerstown, Ohio)

Always choose the right

Be honest

Come on time

Do your work neatly

Enjoy your lessons

Finish your work

Give joy to others

Help one another

In games, join in

Joyfully sing

Keep trying

Listen carefully

Make friends with everybody

Never cheat or mock

Obey all rules

Play fair

Quietly do your work

Respect others

Sit and stand straight

Talk English at school

Use your time wisely

Visit kindly

Welcome visitors

e**X**amine your work

Yell outside only

Zealously do your work

What a fine world it would be if everyone knew this alphabet.

Things that make me smile

Young Amish girls, pedaling their bicycles along the road, their head-covering ribbons fluttering and floating in the air, straight out behind them.

November

What do you say about November? It isn't autumn, and it isn't winter. Most of the trees have lost their leaves. Those leaves that are still holding on are the color of parchment. The fields are bare and brown, with stubble where the field corn has been cut off. They look depressed or rejected. After months of bearing bountiful harvests, now they seem desolate.

Soon the snow will come, cover them with pretty whiteness, and they can sleep. For now, they are bare, brown, stubbly, and almost ugly. What is there to look forward to? Winter? Though I love the beauty of winter, the older I get, the harder it is to welcome winter.

This started out as such a warm November. Delightfully, we hoped autumn would never end, and then suddenly it turned cold. How could we complain? Winter must come, yet this sudden cold seems *so cold*.

The garden is truly finished. Even the weeds have turned brown and dried up. The broccoli continued to grow long after everything else had stopped, then with the sudden cold, even the broccoli had to call it winter.

The sun is setting earlier, so the chickens are going to roost earlier as each day grows shorter. With the garden spent, we will allow the chickens to freely range all over the property, and I can once again enjoy having them by my back door.

What do Amish women do during these shorter November days? Edna has been cleaning up her flower beds. Oh, how I need to do that! Ruth has been canning chicken soup. Don't we have that recipe? *Mommie* and Rachel have been canning pumpkin. I had to can some pumpkin myself this autumn, when I ran out of freezer space. But I won't soon run out of pumpkin. Even though we ran a "Pumpkin Lovers' Special" for the Bed & Breakfast, jars and jars of pumpkin still line my basement shelves.

―――――――――

It is a drizzly, dreary, colorless November day. The trees are dark and leafless, silhouetted against a pale slate gray, sad sky. Dirty smudges of clouds, looking like wisps of smoke, hang so low it seems as if one could touch them, except I'm not sure one would want to. Would my hand come away dirty? In the fields with corn shocks, the shocks no longer look golden and pleasant to the eye; instead they are the color of oatmeal. Not freshly cooked oatmeal, but oatmeal that has sat in the pot overnight.

Not a nice day to be driving about? No, it is the perfect day for us to bring a little happiness, fellowship, fun, and food to two ladies. My Amish sisters have put aside this day to visit a sister-in-law and an aunt, both who are recently widowed. We will have "Morning Coffee" with one and lunch with the other. By the end of the day we will all be filled with pleasant food and even more pleasant memories.

Driving home that evening I see an Amish farmer cutting the corn stubble from out of a field, and gathering it in a wagon.

"What will he do with that," I ask Deborah.

"If he grinds it up, he can use it for bedding in the stalls, and save on straw."

Rachel says she is cold, so I try to explain to her how to operate the heater control, which is in the back of the van.

She studies it quietly for a few seconds, then says, "It doesn't tell me where to put the logs in."

There's a dusting of snow on the ground that wasn't there earlier in the day. Isn't it too early for snow? The sky has turned to slate blue, the color of sky when snow is coming. The field beside us, which some industrious farmer has already plowed in readiness for spring, has deep brown furrows that look like chocolate cake with powdered sugar sprinkled on top. Mmmmm!

Going to an auction in November can be chancy, weather wise. Will it be cold? Will it pour down rain? This morning was November Gray, but not quite cold. It was not raining, but the sky looked very threatening.

Amish seem to love auctions. Many appear to go for the fun of it, more than for what they can buy. They bring their own chairs and settle in for the day. The lunch wagon will do a brisk business, as most Amish will eat a full meal before the auction is over. Children run and play, while the adults stand close to what they are interested in buying.

I had to laugh when I looked around and noticed that the *Englich* men were all standing around the automobile which was to be auctioned off, the Amish men were all examining the garden tools, and the Amish women were all standing patiently waiting for the auctioneer to start the bidding on the boxes of canning jars. I wasn't sure where I needed to stand. We had been looking to buy another car, and I needed a new hoe for the garden since mine had just broken, but can't I always use more canning jars? *(See page 100)*

Jordan

Jordan is ten pounds of mischief, ten pounds of curiosity, and a few more pounds of just little boy. He has hair the color of wheat on a hot summer day and eyes the color of the sky on that same day. When something attracts his attention, the thinking involved is clearly written on his face. It is as if you can almost hear the wheels turning inside his head asking, "What is that?" "What does it do?" "How does it work?" "If I tear it apart, will I be able to tell how it works?"

Putting it back together isn't necessarily important to this boy's thought process.

Jordan will grow up without electricity, TV, radio, computers, video games, or being driven daily in a car to day care or soccer practice. Very seldom will he get a Happy Meal from McDonald's, and maybe never will he eat it in front of a DVD player, which is playing a Walt Disney movie.

Jordan will spend his childhood with a stay-at-home Mom, who prepares his meals three times a day with homegrown vegetables and farm-raised meat. His Mom will read to him while he sits on her lap, play with him, talk to him, take him for walks, bake cookies that did not come out of a tube, and instruct and discipline him until he grows into a fine, responsible, Christian, Amish man.

Jordan's Mom seems infinitely patient as she tells the latest story of her son's adventures. While describing what he was up to yesterday, what he broke the day before, what he poured out on the barn floor just this morning, and what he climbed into only the other day, there isn't a whisper of anger in her voice; instead there is a smile on her lips and love shining out of her eyes. Numerous times, as she tells her tales, I'm thinking, "I would tan his hide!"

When Jordan's *Daed* (the "Amish" word for Dad) is home, Jordan becomes *Daed's* shadow. Whatever *Daed* wants to do, Jordan will be trying to do also. Feeding the stock, cutting wood, working in the fields, or building something are all opportunities to spend time with *Daed* and learn.

At the end of the day, having worked all day, *Daed* may want to sit, rest, and perhaps look at a hunting catalog. Jordan will most likely be on his lap, pointing at pictures and asking questions.

Jordan has an older sister who is a teenager. It would seem she would be jealous or "put out" with this little intruder. She is a beautiful girl, both inside and out, for she dotes on Jordan much as most teenage girls would dote on a popular Hollywood heartthrob, never seeming to tire of him.

Jordan holds a special place in my heart because he and I have something in common. Though we were both born *Englich,* we have both been adopted into this Amish family. It was, in fact, Jordan's Mom who suggested, "Well, we'll just have to adopt you and make you a sister."

Though my adoption is not official, his is. I was there in the courtroom the day his adoption took place when he was eighteen months old. I had driven a van load of his soon-to-be relatives to join in the celebration. Jordan sat on *Daed's* lap, oblivious to the procedure that would make him a part of a world set apart; different from the world most of us live in. Some would think he would be deprived. I think he will be abundantly blessed.

I have stood a step or two back and watched this little *Englich* boy become Amish. The first time I saw him out of baby clothes and wearing "little Amish boy pants" with suspenders, I must have stared, for his Mom asked, with pleasure in her voice, "He looks Amish, doesn't he?"

He did!

He speaks "Amish" now and rolls his "Rs" better than I ever will, and like all Amish children he is beginning to learn English. He is a delightful, inquisitive, happy child who makes my heart glad every time I see him.

Just a short time ago, on a November morning, Jordan sat on his *Daed's* lap in the courtroom, again. This time his new sister was being adopted.

Drizzling and almost dark outside, it hardly seemed appropriate weather for such a joyous occasion. It had been a seventeen-month-long exercise in faith, believing that this precious bundle that had been among us since she was only two days old would not be snatched away from us.

Jordan, like his big sister, shows no jealousy or sibling rivalry. Instead he imitates the total acceptance and love that surrounds him.

The judge's approval of this adoption is made abundantly clear in her statement, "Without this adoption, this child would grow up in Godless squalor." I was stunned at her outspokenness.

My heart skipped with joy when the adoption was final, saying over and over, "They can't take her away from us! She's ours now and they can't take her away from us!"

Now Jordan and his sister, instead of being raised in Godless squalor, will be raised in Godly Love, in an Amish home.

For He foreordained us to be adopted as
His own children through Jesus Christ…

Ephesians 1:5 (Amplified)

Jordan's Favorite Cookies

Cream together:
1 cup brown sugar
1 cup white sugar
1 cup butter
1 cup milk
2 eggs
1 tsp. vanilla

Mix together:
5-6 cups flour
5 tsp. baking powder
2 tsp. baking soda
½ tsp. salt
1½ cups chocolate chips, nuts, raisins, M&Ms, or any combination you have on hand.

Combine all ingredients. Drop by rounded spoonfuls onto lightly greased baking sheet. Bake at 350° for 10 minutes. Don't overbake.
Jordan likes his with icing.

Quick Icing

6 Tbsp. butter
4 Tbsp. cream

¾ cup sugar

Mix together in pan; heat until boiling. Boil for two minutes. Remove from heat and cool slightly. Add enough powdered sugar so icing can be easily spread on cookies.

Things that make me smile

A little Amish boy wearing
dirty, black rubber boots, big
enough for his older brother,
coming up past his knees,
walking with a purposeful
stride necessary just to keep
those boots on his feet.

Amish Women

It seems as though I have written about Amish women more than anything in this book, and yet I want to write more. Why? It's as if I want to somehow sum it all up. Then Deborah did it for me.

She and her daughters decided that I needed help. The Bed & Breakfast had kept me so busy that I was just about worn out. They came over and cleaned our house. They made beds, cleaned bathrooms, dusted, vacuumed, mopped, and even brought snacks with coffee.

When I tried to explain how I would not feel right having them do my work, Deborah brushed me off with, "That's what we're here for, to help each other." Oh, I will try to repay them, but that will be an extremely difficult task.

It reminded me of another time, when Rachel and I hosted a garage sale together. During the preparation time of getting everything priced and put out, Rachel asked me several times, "Can I help you with that?"

Having lived alone for so many years before I married Clay, I had become accustomed to doing everything by myself. Each time she asked me, "Can I help you?" I politely replied, "No, thank you," or, "That's okay, I can do it!" To me it seemed wrong to have her do my work when I could do it myself.

After a while I realized that she looked hurt. When I asked her what was the matter, she sadly replied, "You won't let me help you with anything."

My society dictates that I be independent and self-sufficient. I believe they call it "liberated." Her society says we should help each other, share, give of ourselves, and expect nothing in return. They are taught to work as a family or a community, depending upon each other, knowing there is always someone there for them. I'm just wondering, "Who's liberated?"

For a while, Rachel and I made weekly visits to Wooster so she could see a certain doctor. Traveling back and forth, we became close—talking, sharing, and laughing together in spite of our age difference.

Somehow we fell into the habit of always eating lunch at Taco Bell. It was there one lunchtime that the lady at the next table began talking to us. When the lady got up and left, I noticed again that Rachel looked sad.

"What's wrong?" I asked.

Speaking of the lady who had just left, Rachel answered, "She didn't say anything nice about her husband."

"It's called 'Male Bashing'," I answered her sadly.

I will never forget the look on her face when she asked me, "Why would we want to *bash* ourselves in the *head?*"

Why would we, Rachel? It's such a good question. In our quest for *liberation* I fear that we women have come far away from what God intended for us. Ephesians 5:33 says that every man should love his wife, and every wife should respect her husband. There's not much respect in *male bashing,* and it must be hard for a *bashed* man to love she who *bashes* him. Where's the *liberation?*

I see liberation in the Amish women who are provided for, sheltered, kept from the hardest physical labor, loved, and able to live without the threat of divorce hanging over their heads.

I see liberation in the eyes of an Amish mother of seven children, who rejoices with her sister over the birth of her tenth child, and still delights in her turn at holding the newborn as it is passed around the circle of women, each one liberated to display the feminine nurturing that God intended for them to have.

I see liberation, not entrapment, in women being allowed to stay home and lovingly raise their own children.

I see respect in the way that Amish women choose to live their lives according to how they interpret the Bible, respecting not only their husbands, but also their elders, their ministers, their bishops, and each other with their ability to forgive and forget.

I feel respect from every Amish person I know who allows me to be *Englich* and not Amish, and does not make me feel that somehow I am not as good as they are because I am not Amish.

I *think* I hear respect in Fanny's voice when she spoke of coming home from church, telling herself, "I'm going to wear this (church) bonnet all the way home…then it gets so hot…and I can't see… and I can't hear what Roman is saying…so he is shouting at me…"

I see love in the brother and sister who hosted a 25th Anniversary celebration dinner for Clay and me, serving a beautiful, delicious dinner to 24 people, then presenting us with cards, gifts, and money.

I see love every time an Amish man or woman helps a neighbor, church member, sister, or brother in a barn raising, frolic, wedding, or anytime someone needs help.

"I planned on going hunting this morning," he told me, "but I'll go another time. Alan needs help with his fences."

I heard love in *Mommie's* response when I pointed out the house near Wilmot that I had wanted to buy when we were house hunting. "If you had bought that house," she said, "we wouldn't know you."

I see compassion in the women who grieve when the family horse must be traded or put down. Though they are supposed to be farm women to whom an animal is just for use, they are women who love and to whom that animal has become a beloved pet.

I find honesty, truth, and morals everywhere in Amish Country. There are roadside stands, some large, some with only a few vegetables from the garden. Often there will be a donation box and a sign with the suggested price. I remember the garage sale, set up in the basement of a house, with the following sign, "This is a self-service garage sale. Donations only. Proceeds will go to the needy."

And I see humor every time I turn around. I told Leah, while she was eating some milk chocolate, that recent studies indicated that one or two squares of dark chocolate daily were good for women. Leah, looking down at the chocolate in her lap, said, "Well, since this is milk chocolate, I guess I'll have to eat twice as much."

Deborah, who has never seen a Lay's potato chip commercial on TV, laughs and tells us, "When I'm picking strawberries, I can't eat just one."

And which lady was it, when I unthinkingly told her to put something in her pocket (Their dresses have no pockets), grinned and said, "My other dress has the pocket in it?"

I've always considered that God sending Clay and me to Ohio was a reward. I just could never figure out what we did "good enough" to deserve such a reward. Now I can't figure out what I did to deserve sharing the lives of these truly praiseworthy Amish women.

"God, help me to keep doing 'good' that I might continue to be blessed, and help me to grow toward Ephesians 5:33, that I might have all that You intend for me."

It was thus that Sarah obeyed Abraham (following his guidance and acknowledging his headship over her by) calling him lord—master, leader, authority... Finally, all (of you) should be of one and the same mind (united in spirit), sympathizing (with one another), loving (each the other) as brethren (of one household), compassionate and courteous— tenderhearted and humble-minded.

I Peter 3:6 & 8 (Amplified)

Things that make me smile

Awakening to the clip-clop of horses' hoofs coming up the road, getting gradually louder and louder, passing my house, then becoming softer and softer, fading from my morning.

Amish Wal-Marts

Though most Amish women *love* to shop at Wal-Mart, sometime before Christmas, most of them will also want to visit some of the old-fashioned, small country general stores that can be found on small back roads in Amish Country. If you see one of these while visiting us, you should definitely stop for a visit. What a treat awaits you. It is truly a step back in time to a *Little House on the Prairie* General Store, such as the Olsens owned. We call them "Amish Wal-Marts."

Often, I drive *Mommie* with her sisters and sisters-in-law for a day's outing. They like to start *early*, eat breakfast out, and then drive to different "Amish Wal-Marts." I think for them it is like going back in time, to shop as they did when they were young and these were the only stores available to Amish women.

These country stores are in the middle of nowhere, miles from anything. Like the garage sales, they might be behind the barn, around the corner of the chicken pen…nowhere near the road, and if you don't know it's there, you may not find it. Most of them do not have electricity, and on dark days, the gas lights just don't seem sufficient to this *Englich* lady who is spoiled by electric lights. One time I entered such a store to find a few electric (probably generator-run) lights, only dimly lighting the store. The lady behind the counter got up and began turning on extra lights. I wondered if she did that only for *Englich* customers. However, the lack of light is soon forgotten with the excitement of stepping back in time fifty to one hundred years.

Where shall I begin? Immediately to my right is a wall of socks. Every size one could imagine is available, but in only three colors: black, navy, or gray. Next to the socks are *kappa* (Amish women's coverings) and men's hats. Again, there is little color choice; men's hats are black; *kappa* are white. Then I spot a more modern hat section. Some traditional Amish men's hats have been moved to an upper shelf, and the warmer, more modern sock hat now has the best-selling shelf space. The color choices are again black, navy, or gray. Gloves are next to the sock hats; the only color choice is black. Something you don't find much of in the *Englich* Wal-Marts is a large selection of reflectors and reflector tape to be worn over clothing while walking down the road at night. Being a driver who has come over a hill at night and suddenly realizes that there are people I can hardly see walking by the side of the road, I hope they sell a lot of these reflective articles.

In the hardware section, mailboxes stand next to cans of paint. (There are only ten choices of paint.) Tape measures, hammers, and other tools hang above. Garden tools of every description have a place of honor next to "Amish clothes dryers" (folding clothes racks). Duct tape and wire of all gauges fill in all the small spaces. In one old hardware store that we went into, I instantly thought, "This smells like a Hardware Store." Then I thought, "What does a Hardware Store smell like?"

Flashlights! I have never seen so many flashlights! Coleman lanterns and coolers are on a shelf above the kitchen knives. Is there a kitchen tool you remember your mother or grandmother using, but can't seem to buy anymore? Most likely you could find it here. Choppers, grinders (Amish food processors), mixers, eggbeaters, or strainers, but none of them electric. Ladles the size of soup bowls. Pots big enough to bathe the family cat in. How much soup would that hold? How many people would you feed? Rolling pins that cost a pretty penny, but will definitely be used until their cost is no longer remembered. Canning supplies take up a large section of the kitchen department. Kettles and jars in assorted sizes, some larger than I knew were available. Bands and seals for jars come in large quantities; four dozen seals to a bag.

Close to the kitchen department, I find an assortment of fine china. Like all women, Amish women enjoy things of beauty. I often think that is why they usually excel in their flower gardens. Since it is frowned upon to have anything too "fancy" in their homes, they have found a way to have beauty. They use God's creations, and have beautiful flower gardens. Still, almost every Amish woman I know has a *shank* (china hutch), usually over in a corner, with some truly pretty china in it, and nearly every "Amish Wal-Mart" carries a selection of china and tea pots, in all sizes. A special occasion for Amish women is often celebrated with a "Tea."

Near the kitchen department are some cookbooks. These are a collection of local recipes. I wonder if they aren't here more for the tourists than for the Amish. There are other books for sale: Christian themes, Bible stories, and Bibles. The Bibles are written in what Amish call *High German*. Next to the books and Bibles are wrapping paper, cards, and stationery. Without the use of e-mail and limited use of phones, the art of letter writing is alive and well in the Amish communities. Therefore a much better selection of stationery is available than in any stores I have found in the *Englich* world. I am delighted to find these selections of stationery, as my 92-year-old mother still loves to write and receive letters.

If you are into stamping, and looking for different rubber stamps, an "Amish Wal-Mart" is the place to look. In fact, supplies for making cards are numerous in most of these stores, as card making is a common hobby among Amish women. School supplies are also in this part of the store, and a small gift selection of knickknacks for those who suddenly remembered that they need a gift and don't want to hire a driver to take them to the nearest *Englich* Wal-Mart.

There is a baby section with both practical items and items worthy of gift giving.

Suddenly I find loose items, in little wooden compartments. A memory from the past flashes across my mind. Isn't this the way merchandise was displayed in the old Five and Dimes of my childhood? Loose items with no bar codes, and a sign that says 10 cents each. Wow! Even the price is out of my childhood!

As Amish women sew their own clothes, their children's clothes, and much of their husband's clothes, fabric takes up a large section of "Amish Wal-Marts." There are rows and rows of fabric with a surprisingly good selection of colors. Out of curiosity I paced out the fabric section in one store and found four rows of fabric bolts, each row about five yards long, and out of all that fabric, only sixteen bolts had any pattern with different colors on them. Amish clothing is made from solid color material, no patterns. However, I have begun to notice a little "stretching" of the rules. Some material, though a solid color, may have a pattern due to the weaving of the thread. Don't most of us want a little variety in our lives? In the fabric section are also all kinds of sewing notions: thread, snaps, needles, pins, elastic, hooks and eyes, and thimbles. (An Amish woman told me once that she *always* carries a thimble.) Some stores might even have a sewing machine for sale. There will be buttons, as buttons are allowed on small girls' dresses until they are old enough to use pins. One time I found buttons displayed in ice cube trays with a sign that read, "4 cents each or 12 for 48 cents." Am I missing something? Where's the savings in buying 12? In the "Wal-Mart we are visiting today I see two older Amish ladies sitting and quilting. What a peaceful way to spend a day!

The toy department is truly a step back into my childhood. Here are toys that don't require batteries, only imagination. They don't beep, whistle, play music, talk, or have any computerized parts. Balls, tops, puzzles, books and games, farm sets, and toy barns. For the girls there are dolls, dishes, miniature kitchen utensils, and everything a little girl needs to imitate Mom. For the boys there are tools like Dad's, as well as tractors, wagons, manure spreaders, and every farm implement John Deere has ever manufactured. All are made in strong, durable metal to last through a rough childhood of play and perhaps even be passed on to the next generation. And horses! There are dozens of horses in every size and in more color choices than we found in the sock department. Oh, look at this! A View Master. How many hours did I spend as a child looking through a View Master, dreaming of places and envisioning stories?

My favorite place to shop is the "pharmacy." It is generally contained entirely upon a shelf or two, near the front of the store. Salves, ointments, liniment, peppermint oil (What do you do with peppermint oil?), and lotions crowd the shelf. One bottle states "Serious hand lotion for hands that do serious work." There's castor oil, and wintergreen oil, and tins of salve for your aches, burns, and bruises; Skinner's Salve (vaporizing), Burchicks Salve (it's all natural), TO-MOR-GONE Salve (a black salve that is a natural herbal remedy), Union Salve, Draw Salve, and my favorite name, Tobacco Lung Fever Salve. How could one ever decide which salve to use? Syrups for your coughs and colds, or how about Kruse Original Save the Baby Cough Suppressant? Here you find items with the quaintest names; Bag Balm, Poho Oil, Dr. Ruggles Skin Restorer, Grandpa Balsam's Dietary Supplement, or Grandma's Old-Fashioned Cholera Balsam. Read this one: R.E.P. "A blend of oils having many uses. For sinus infection, put on forehead and cheeks. For breath freshener, put drop on tongue." Here's B & W Ointment for burns and wounds. Isn't that what the salves were for? Or we could try Amish Origins-Old Time Chickweed Salve or Amish Origins-Deep Penetrating Pain Relief. A large bottle was labeled, "White Liniment." It was pink. A smaller bottle also labeled "White Liniment" was almost black. Do I not know the definition of the word "white"? Perhaps we can eliminate the need for any of these by simply taking Hostetler's Herbal Super Tonic. If you believe these labels, it would seem as though there is a cure for anything!

I know of one "Amish Wal-Mart" that has recently expanded to carry bulk foods, spices, dairy, deli meats and cheese, and quite a selection of other groceries. Does this make it a "*Super* Amish Wal-Mart?"

Who can find a virtuous woman? for her price is far above rubies… She seeketh wool and flax, and worketh willingly with her hands… She perceiveth that her merchandise is good: her candle goeth not out by night.

Proverbs 31:10-18

Things that make me smile

The breath of horses, billowing
out from their nostrils on
frigid winter mornings, like
steam from a steam engine;
trailing behind them as
they travel down the road,
and hanging for a moment,
like a cloud; proof that
something hardworking
has passed this way.

December

It's cold! Why am I picking up Amish women at 6:30 on a December morning? Should it be this cold, this early in December? The winter sky is dull and cold looking, with little sign of sunlight. See, it's so early even the sun doesn't want to get up yet. Wait! Streaks of brightest pink slowly begin to appear. They enlarge and multiply with each second, making me think, "Perhaps it *is* time to be up and enjoying God's beauty." A fence to my right catches the morning light. How can *every* wire on that chicken wire fence be covered with frost? How long did it take Jack Frost to do that? He must have had help. It looks like fancy Spanish lace. If only I could bring it inside my home and put it on my dining room table.

A horse and buggy pass by. The *frost whiskers* on the horse are *so* long. The Amish say, "The longer the whiskers, the longer the journey."

A *Daudi*, walking along the road, carries sacks from the local "general store." His breath billows out in front of him, giving testimony to how cold it is. Cows in the fields stand in groups around hay bales, eating hay that has been placed there for them.

By the time I've picked up Rachel, the sun is a ball of fire, just cresting a snow-covered hill. "Look, wouldn't you like a slice of that?"

"It looks like it is made out of orange or lemon," Rachel says.

"Would it taste like citrus?" I wonder.

"Yes," she answers, "but it would have to taste like a *hot* citrus drink."

On a snowy December morning, I passed an old Amish man with a young boy, hauling a church wagon to the next farm that will host church services. It is so cold that the old man sits hunched over, trying to conserve as much heat as possible against the falling snow and blowing wind. Though his wide-brimmed hat is pulled low, his worn face still reveals how many times it has faced the weather. His expression tells that this is a job to be done, no matter the conditions, so let's just get it done.

The young boy is a study in the opposite. Instead of hunching over against the cold, he leans forward in anticipation of the adventure. His hat is set back on his head, perhaps so he won't miss seeing anything along the way. A little cold and snow aren't going to stop him from enjoying this opportunity to sit on top of the world and watch it parade by just for his pleasure.

On Christmas morning I awoke to a world where everything was white or gray. The ground, the fields, the sky were all white. The faint outline of hills in the distance and the sleeping cherry tree outside my window were all gray. No color! Then a small pink smudge appeared in the sky, evidence of a sun trying to shine through the gray.

I heard the horse's hoofs on the road long before I could see the horse and buggy. I waited with anticipation. After living among the Amish for so long, I was pleased that I could still find pleasure in watching a buggy go by. And what pleasure! The horse and buggy was a stark, black silhouette against the backdrop of white and gray. The sun had finally found a place to shine through, full and golden above the gray smudges of hills on the horizon, and a million sparkles suddenly appeared all over my world. Does snow sparkle more in Ohio?

The horse held his head high and tossed his mane with delight and assurance, as if he was so happy just to be alive on Christmas morning. I smiled. Soon there would be the hustle and bustle of gifts around the tree, followed by dinner to cook for old friends that were coming to join us, but for that moment, all was peaceful, quiet, white and gray, golden and sparkly. For like the horse, I too was happy just to be alive in Amish Country on such a Christmas morning.

Clay and I were first drawn to Amish Country because we felt a peace every time we came. Year after year, thousands of tourists flock to Amish Country to catch a glimpse of a lifestyle they long to become a part of. Feeling they are missing something in their own lives, they think they see it in the Amish with their seemingly contented existence.

"There's something missing in my life…"

"I can't quite find happiness…"

"There must be a way to have more peace…"

Yes, the Amish have a wonderful lifestyle. We can learn much from them, but don't believe that being Amish is the answer to your search.

We are all looking to "fill a hole;" a "hole" that says, "Something is not quite right in my life." That hole can only be filled with one thing—*GOD!*

To become Amish seems like a tangible solution, but becoming Amish doesn't necessarily make you a Christian any more than moving into a garage would make you a car. Neither does being born Amish automatically make you a Christian any more than if a mama cat had her kittens in an oven, they would automatically be biscuits.

There is only one way to become a Christian and forever fill that hole in your heart. That way is to accept Jesus Christ as your Lord and Savior. Confess your sins and accept that He died on the cross for your sins, your failures, your shortcomings, and your depression. He endured it all for your salvation, your peace, your joy, your healing, and your deliverance. Because He was our sacrifice, we are promised a place in heaven with Him for eternity. He loved us enough to suffer untold agony so that we would not have to suffer. All that is ours simply for the asking.

From this day forward *(write today's date* _____ *)*, because you have confessed Jesus Christ as your Lord and Savior, you are saved, set free, and on your way to heaven. Yes, you will make mistakes, but you are now instantly forgiven with the simple words, "Father, forgive me." You are now His child whom He wants to not only forgive but wants to bless daily with everything your heart has been longing for.